Third International Workshop on Automatic Translation for Signed and Spoken Languages (AT4SSL 2025)

Geneva, Switzerland
24 June 2025

ISBN: 979-8-3313-2670-8

Printed from e-media with permission by:

Curran Associates, Inc.
57 Morehouse Lane
Red Hook, NY 12571

Some format issues inherent in the e-media version may also appear in this print version.

Association for Computational Linguistics
209 N. Eighth Street
Stroudsburg, Pennsylvania 18360

Phone: 1-570-476-8006
Fax: 1-570-476-0860

acl@aclweb.org

Additional copies of this publication are available from:

Curran Associates, Inc.
57 Morehouse Lane
Red Hook, NY 12571 USA
Phone: 845-758-0400
Fax: 845-758-2633
Email: curran@proceedings.com
Web: www.proceedings.com

at4ssl 2025

AT4SSL

Third International Workshop on Automatic Translation for Signed and Spoken Languages (AT4SSL)

Proceedings of the Workshop

June 24, 2025

Geneva, Switzerland

Message from the Organising Committee

This volume contains the proceedings of the Third International Workshop on Automatic Translation for Signed and Spoken Languages (AT4SSL 2025)[1], collocated with the 20th Machine Translation Summit[2]. For a third time, this one-day workshop provides a platform for researchers and practitioners with background and expertise in sign language linguistics, machine translation, natural language processing, interpreting, image and video recognition, virtual signers synthesis, usability, ethics and others to present and discuss (complete, ongoing or future) research on automatic translation between signed and spoken languages.

AT4SSL 2021 & AT4SSL 2023 The first edition of the AT4SSL workshop[3] was co-located with the AMTA conference in 2021. The workshop was conducted online and was attended by approximately 35 participants. The goal of the first edition of the workshop was to discuss the dichotomy between the fields of machine translation and sign language processing (including SL linguistics, image and video recognition, etc.) and to promote the communication and collaboration between researchers from different (sub)fields aiming at a common goal. The second edition of AT4SSL was co-located with the EAMT 2023 conference. This edition was conducted face-to-face. The main theme of the 2023 edition of the AT4SSL workshop was SL data (as data being one of the key factors for the success of today's AI).

Submissions and programme As with the previous editions, the AT4SSL 2025 welcomed two types of contributions: long and short research papers. We received a total of 6 new submissions (all of which long papers). Following the peer-review process, 4 submissions were accepted, resulting in an acceptance rate of 67%.

The accepted papers cover diverse topics. The paper by Amit Moryossef, Gerard Sant and Zifan Jiang describes a method to alter the appearance of a signer (in a recorded or digitised signed utterance) using pose estimation and a generative adversarial network (GAN). This work aids the task of anonymising signed language videos. The work of Bastien David, Pierrette Bouillon, Jonathan Mutal, Irene Strasly, Johanna Gerlach and Hervé Spechbach contributes with a new parallel sign language translation corpus in the medical domain. This corpus includes French (as source language), LSF-CH videos (as target) and the G-SiGML code to those LSF-CH videos. The G-SiGML is automatically generated using the SIGLA[4] rule-based system. Naiara Gamendia, Horacio Saggion and Euan McGill present in their paper novel approaches for Spontaneous Isolated Sign Language Recognition for Catalan Sign Language (LSC) along with the first dataset of isolated signs derived from an available LSC corpus. In contrast to the aforementioned three works, the one of Lisa Lepp, Mirella De Sisto and Dimitar Shterionov looks into, on the one hand, the user and, on the other hand, the (typical) machine translation pipeline and its phases. Based on existing literature (111 articles), it uncovers the amount of users and their roles in each of the typical phases of a machine translation project, aiming to provide more insights on user-involvement and co-creation in SLMT projects.

AT4SSL 2025 features Gomèr Otterspeer as keynote speaker. Gomèr Otterspeer, a Software Engineer at the SignLab team at the University of Amsterdam, is one of the Deaf team members of the SignLab with primary role in collaboration with researchers to co-create technology, raise awareness about Deaf culture, and promote the use of Sign Language through programming and advisory roles in related projects. The keynote presentation features a novel project on translating text to SL for patient leaflets. The research specifically focuses on reusing existing SL animation videos, replacing only one sign or a short sequence within a sentence, ensuring efficient and consistent communication.

[1] https://sites.google.com/tilburguniversity.edu/at4ssl2025

[2] https://mtsummit2025.unige.ch/

[3] https://aclanthology.org/volumes/2021.mtsummit-at4ssl/

[4] https://babeldr.unige.ch/demos-and-resources#sigla

Acknowledgments This workshop is sponsored by Tilburg University's Cognitive Science and Artificial Intelligence (CSAI) department,[5] the Sector Plan for Social Sciences and Humanities,[6] theme Human AI & Datafied Society and SignLab[7] at the University of Amsterdam.

We sincerely thank everyone that contributed to and supported this edition of the AT4SSL workshop: the authors of the submitted papers for their interest in the topic, the Programme Committee members for their valuable feedback and insightful comments, the CSAI department (TiU) and the SIgnLab (UvA), and the MT Summit organizers, with special thanks to Ms Lise Volkart and Dr Sabrina Girletti.

We hope you enjoy reading the papers and we are looking forward to a fruitful and enriching workshop!

Dimitar Shterionov
Mirella De Sisto
Bram Vanroy
Vincent Vandeghinste
Victoria Nyst
Myriam Vermeerbergen
Floris Roelofsen
Lisa Lepp
Irene Strasly

[5] https://www.tilburguniversity.edu/about/schools/tshd/departments/dca
[6] https://www.sectorplan-ssh.nl
[7] https://www.signlab-amsterdam.nl/

Organising Committee

Dimitar Shterionov	Department of Cognitive Science and Artificial Intelligence, Tilburg School of Humanities and Digital Sciences, Tilburg University, The Netherlands
Mirella De Sisto	Department of Cognitive Science and Artificial Intelligence, Tilburg School of Humanities and Digital Sciences, Tilburg University, The Netherlands
Vincent Vandeghinste	Faculty of Arts, KU Leuven, Belgium; Instituut voor de Nederlandse Taal (Dutch Language Institute), The Netherlands
Victoria Nyst	Centre for Linguistics, Faculty of Humanities, Leiden University, The Netherlands
Myriam Vermeerbergen	Faculty of Arts, KU Leuven (campus Antwerp), Belgium
Floris Roelofsen	Institute for Logic, Language and Computation, University of Amsterdam, The Netherlands
Bram Vanroy	Faculty of Arts, KU Leuven, Belgium; Instituut voor de Nederlandse Taal (Dutch Language Institute), The Netherlands
Lisa Lepp	Department of Cognitive Science and Artificial Intelligence, Tilburg School of Humanities and Digital Sciences, Tilburg University, The Netherlands
Irene Strasly	Faculty of Translation and Interpretation, University of Geneva, Switzerland

Programme Committee

Ioannis Tsochantaridis	Google Research, Switzerland
Amit Moryossef	Bar-Ilan University, Israel; sign.mt
Lyke Esselink	University of Amsterdam, the Netherlands
Joni Dambre	Ghent University, Belgium
Maartje De Meulder	HU University of Applied Sciences Utrecht, the Netherlands; Honorary fellow at Heriot-Watt University, the UK
Caner Doğan	Middle East Technical University, the Republic of Türkiye
Sarah Ebling	University of Zurich, Switzerland
Abraham Glasser	Gallaudet University in Washington, USA
Euan McGill	Universitat Pompeu Fabra, Spain
Jonathan Mutal	University of Geneva, Switzerland
Oline Ranum	University of Amsterdam, the Netherlands
Daniel Stein	eBay Inc., Germany
Rosalee Wolfe	DePaul University, USA

Keynote Talk

Blending Sentences with Avatar Advanced Sign Language Animation Technology

Gomèr Otterspeer
SignLab, University of Amsterdam

Abstract: In this talk, we explore how automatic translation from written text to Sign Language of the Netherlands (NGT) can be effectively applied in contexts requiring large volumes of accessible information, such as the medical sector. Patient leaflets, for example, often contain thousands of sentences that differ only slightly from one another. Our research specifically focuses on reusing existing sign language animation videos, replacing only one sign or a short sequence within a sentence, ensuring efficient and consistent communication.

For example:

Original Sentence	Variation Example
1 in 10,000 people experience a serious side effect (n=100)	1 in 10,000 people experience a headache.
1 in 10,000 people experience a serious side effect (n=100)	1 in 100 people experience a serious side effect.

Our approach involves processing sign language sentences captured using motion capture technology. These captured motions are then applied to avatars created with Ready Player Me to generate animated videos, which are displayed in our Babylon 3D viewer tool. To accurately identify and segment specific signs within sentences, we utilize a semi-automated annotation tool. This annotation allows for precise and natural replacement of targeted segments within sign language video clips.

Subsequently, we validate our method by conducting focus group sessions. Participants in these groups perform blind tests, viewing various sentences and determining whether each sentence is a naturally recorded video or a hybrid composition. This ensures that our automated sign replacement maintains clarity, naturalness, and user comprehension.

This is a promising method for scalable, efficient, and user-friendly sign language translation, bridging accessibility gaps through careful integration of annotation technology, motion capture, and attention to visual grammar and user feedback.

Bio: Gomèr Otterspeer is currently employed as a Software Engineer in the SignLab team at the University of Amsterdam. He is one of the Deaf team members of the SignLab with primary role in collaboration with researchers to co-create technology, raise awareness about Deaf culture, and promote the use of Sign Language through programming and advisory roles in related projects.

Since 2024, Gomèr work is focused on specialized areas including Artificial Intelligence (AI), Motion Capture, and Dataset Management. Over the past year, the SignLab team he is part of has collected an extensive dataset consisting of more than 24,000 recordings, each captured from five distinct perspectives. Furthermore, the lab works on motion capturing with which they have collected more than 5,000 recordings.

Gomèr's current objective is to curate this data into a comprehensive dataset of the Dutch Sign Language (NGT) for publication purposes, and subsequently utilize it to train AI models aimed at automating annotation.

Table of Contents

Pose-Based Sign Language Appearance Transfer

Amit Moryossef[1, 2*], Gerard Sant[1*], Zifan Jiang[1]
[1]University of Zurich, [2]sign.mt
amit@sign.mt

Abstract

We introduce a method for transferring the signer's appearance in sign language skeletal poses while preserving the sign content. Using estimated poses, we transfer the appearance of one signer to another, maintaining natural movements and transitions. This approach improves pose-based rendering and sign stitching while obfuscating identity. Our experiments show that while the method reduces signer identification accuracy, it slightly harms sign recognition performance, highlighting a tradeoff between privacy and utility. Our code is available at `https://github.com/sign-language-processing/pose-anonymization`.

1 Introduction

Personal data, particularly person-identifying information, is central to data protection laws in many countries, including the EU General Data Protection Regulation (GDPR; European Parliament and Council of the European Union (2016)). In signed languages, identifying information is embedded in every utterance through appearance, prosody, movement patterns, and sign choices (Bragg et al., 2020; Battisti et al., 2024). Therefore, from an information-theoretic perspective, removing all identifying information necessitates removing all information. However, a tradeoff between privacy and utility can be achieved by selectively removing some information.

We propose a straightforward yet effective method for altering the appearance of a signer in a sign language pose (Figure 1) while preserving the underlying sign content (§3). Specifically, given a sign language video by signer α and an image of person β, our method generates the appearance of person β performing the same signs as signer α.

Qualitatively, this method effectively smooths skeletal pose stitching (Moryossef et al., 2023b), and improves pose-based video rendering (Saunders et al., 2021). However, quantitative evaluation of our method as data augmentation reveals that while it can help confuse signer identification models, it hurts sign language recognition (§5).

2 Related Work

Research on sign language poses appearance varies in purpose. As Isard (2020) highlights, video anonymization falls into two main categories: concealing parts of the video (Hanke et al., 2020; Rust et al., 2024) or reproducing the video without certain information. This work focuses on the latter.

For instance, Saunders et al. (2021) replace the signer's visual appearance, targeting human consumption. They estimate poses from the original

Figure 1: The average MediaPipe Holistic frame (landmarks reduced for visual clarity) extracted from a large sign language dataset ($\approx$ 50 million frames).

video and use a Generative Adversarial Network (GAN; Goodfellow et al. (2014)) to generate a different-looking human. This process, working correctly, anonymizes the signing video as effectively as pose estimation alone, since all of the information from the original pose is captured and reproduced. Similarly, cartoon-based anonymization methods replicate signing with animated avatars but often miss key details like facial expressions and hand configurations (Tze et al., 2022).

Battisti et al. (2024) found that pose estimation alone does not conceal signer identity. They noted signers could still be recognized from pose data, highlighting the need for advanced anonymization techniques to better protect privacy. Our work addresses this gap by proposing an appearance transfer to help obfuscate sign language poses.

3 Method

Our appearance transfer approach focuses on altering the appearance of the signer in a pose sequence while preserving the underlying sign information. The method assumes that the video starts from a relaxed posture, not mid-signing.

Given a pose sequence by signer α (P_α), and a single pose frame by signer β (P_β), both poses are normalized to a common scale based on shoulder width, using the `pose-format` (Moryossef et al., 2021a) library. The appearance of both signers is assumed to exist in the first frame of each pose.

Ignoring the hands, to transfer the appearance of signer β to the video by signer α, we modify the pose sequence by removing the appearance of α and adding the appearance of β (Equation 1).

$$\hat{P_\alpha} = P_\alpha - P_\alpha^0 + P_\beta^0 \tag{1}$$

To perform a standardized anonymization, we choose person β as the mean frame in a large sign language dataset (Figure 1). This results in an average proportioned human, which does not specifically look similar to any individual person. We note that from an information-theoretic perspective, this approach does not guarantee anonymity. Usage is depicted in Algorithm 1.

4 Qualitative Evaluation

This simple approach yields outstanding results. To start, we show a few pose frames from different poses, when transferred to the mean appearance (anonymized) and when transferred to the appearance of a different person (Table 1).

Algorithm 1 'Anonymizing' a pose sequence

```
from pose_format import Pose
from pose_anonymization.appearance \
    import remove_appearance

with open("example.pose", "rb") as f:
  pose = Pose.read(f.read())

pose = remove_appearance(pose)
```

We consider a recent paper on sign language stitching and rendering (Moryossef et al., 2023b). This paper translates spoken language text to sign language videos by identifying relevant signs from a lexicon, stitching them together in a smart way (cropping neutral positions and smoothing the transition), and then rendering a video using a rendering model, trained on a single interpreter. We introduce a single intervention—after finding relevant lexicon items, we transfer the appearance of the pose to be the pose of the interpreter the renderer was trained on.

Rendering The rendering model is a Stable Diffusion model (Rombach et al., 2021) fine-tuned using ControlNet (Zhang and Agrawala, 2023) for controllability from poses. Since the model was trained on the appearance of a single person, it is not robust to various appearances as an input. Generally, it is not a great model, and we would like to maximize the results we get from it. Figure 2 demonstrates the rendering of the face of the original vs. the new pose. We can see that when transferring to the appearance of the interpreter the model was trained on, the results are more 'human'.

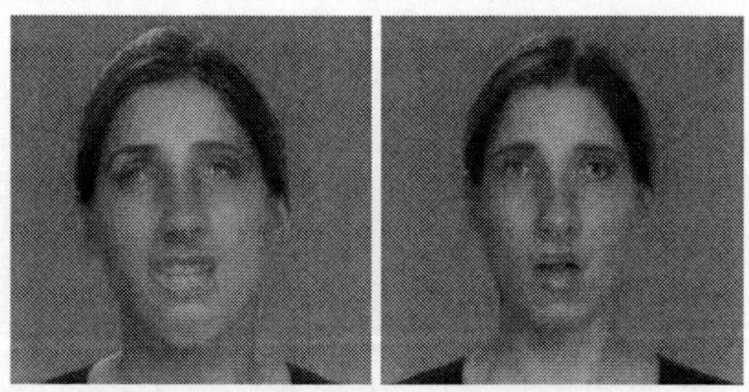

(a) Without transfer (b) With transfer

Figure 2: Faces from ControlNet Rendering

Sign Stitching Given a uniform appearance, the stitched pose sequence is now more coherent and less jumpy. The size of different body parts does not change during the sentence, and the stitching points look smoother. When tracking optical flow

Sign	Original	Anonymized	Transferred
Kleine ('small')	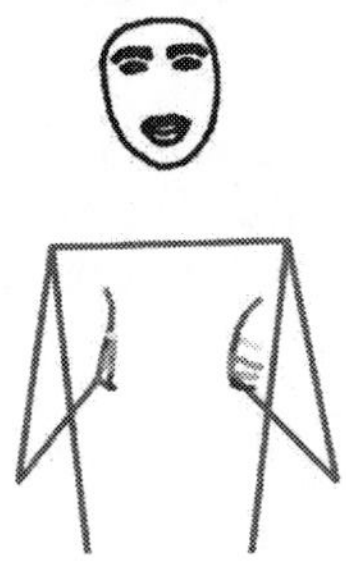	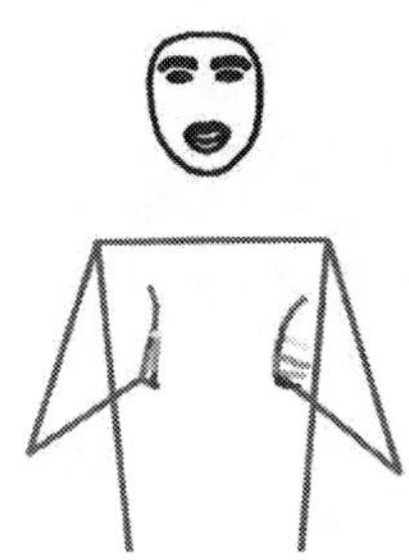	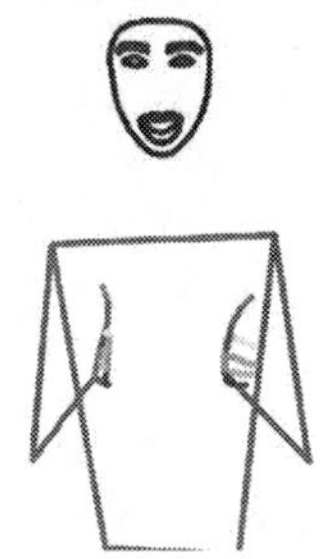
Kinder ('children')			
essen ('eat')	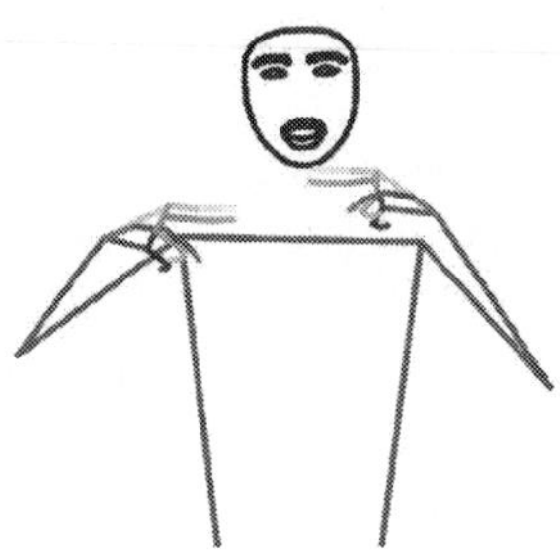	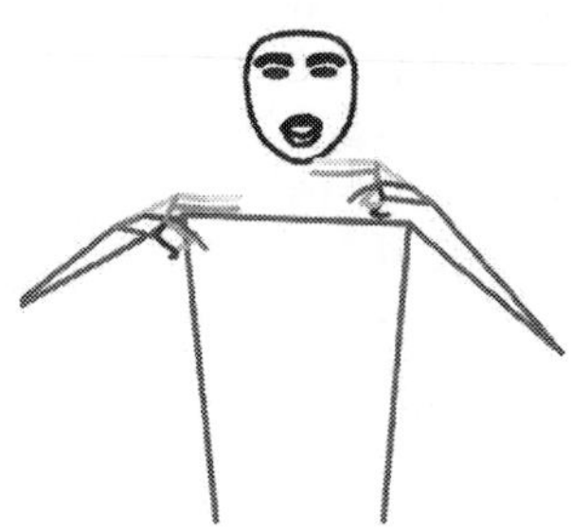	
Pizza ('pizza')		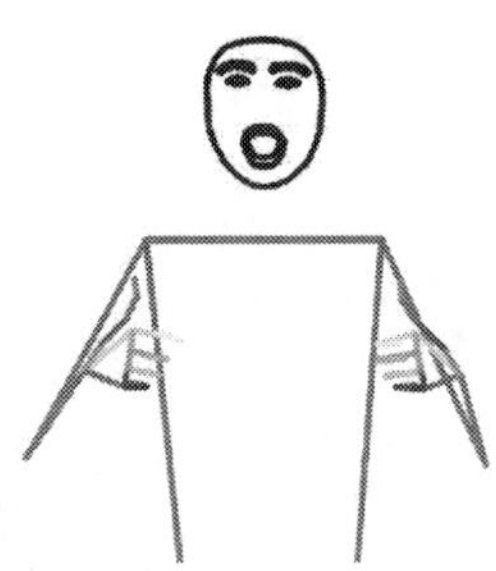	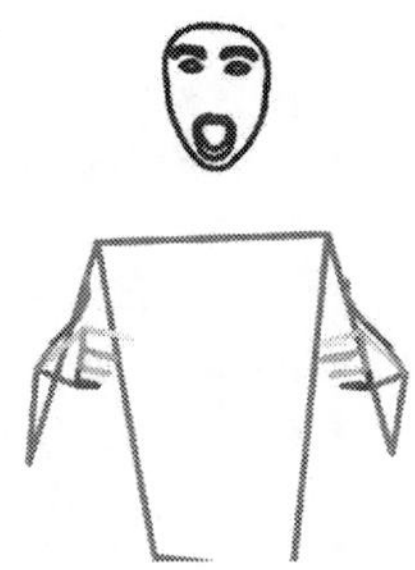

Table 1: Example of four signs. On the left, we show the middle frame from the original sign. In the middle, an anonymized version using an average pose from a large sign language dataset. On the right, appearance is transferred to be of a specific interpreter. For a video comparison, check out `https://github.com/sign-language-processing/pose-anonymization`.

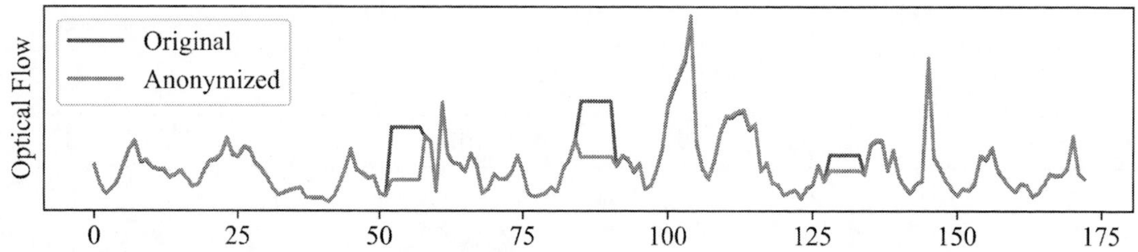

Figure 3: Optical flow (the magnitude of change between two frames) for a stitched video from four original videos and anonymized videos. Higher values represent a larger local change, and a higher area under the curve represents a larger change overall. The flow is exactly the same for all frames except for the stitching zones.

across the pose sequence (Figure 3), sign transitions are smoother and less noticeable, when comparing the use of anonymized and original poses.

5 Experiments and Results

To quantify the effect of our appearance transfer method on sign language recognition, we used the code provided by Moryossef et al. (2021b) for both sign and signer recognition tasks. We hypothesized that transferred poses could serve as an effective data augmentation technique, allowing us to train models to a similar quality while obfuscating signer identities during both training and testing phases.

For our experiments, we used the AUTSL dataset (Sincan and Keles, 2020), which includes 226 distinct lexical sign classes. Importantly, the appearance transfer process did not modify hand pose features, focusing instead on the body and face.

We trained the model under four conditions: (1) using the original pose sequences; (2) applying a single appearance transfer to the average pose shown in Figure 1; (3) transferring multiple appearances for each sample; and (4) combining all these data sources, with 10% original poses, 10% average poses, and 80% transferred appearances. During testing, each model was evaluated on the original pose sequences, transferred to the average pose, and transferred to 10 distinct appearances, with the latter utilizing majority voting, referred to as the *Transferred* method.

As shown in Table 2, no configuration outperformed the model trained and tested with the original pose sequences (top-left). However, training on a combination of original and transferred poses made the model more robust in inference on appearance-augmented data (bottom-right).

To evaluate the extent to which our appearance transfer method obfuscates signer identity, we retrained the model using the original pose sequences but replaced the final sign classification layer with a signer classification layer, freezing the rest of the network as per Sant and Escolano (2023).

Train	Test		
	Original	**Anonymized**	**Transferred**
(1) Original Poses	**80.97%**	65.82%	71.46%
(2) Anonymized Poses	63.26%	64.48%	51.50%
(3) Transferred Poses	67.08%	66.54%	57.32%
(4) Combined	79.96%	60.88%	76.78%

Table 2: Sign recognition accuracy on the AUTSL test set. 'Transferred' is an ensemble of predictions from the same 10 different appearances selected randomly.

When trained and tested on the original poses, the model achieved 80.18% accuracy in identifying the signer, demonstrating the existence of identifiable traits. When trained and tested on anonymized poses, accuracy dropped to 65.34%, and with transferred poses, it fell further to 52.20%. These results indicate that while our method significantly reduces identifiable information, it does not eliminate it, as random chance would yield only 3.23% accuracy.

6 Conclusions

We presented a method for appearance transfer in sign language poses, allowing the alteration of a signer's appearance within a pose sequence while preserving essential signing information. By normalizing poses and selectively transferring appearance from another individual—excluding hand geometry to maintain natural movement—we achieved smooth and coherent results in sign rendering and stitching tasks.

Our qualitative evaluation shows that the appearance transfer effectively smooths pose transitions and enhances the visual coherence of stitched sign sequences. However, the quantitative results indicate that while the method helps anonymize signer identity, it can negatively impact sign language recognition performance.

Limitations

We believe that the balance between privacy and utility is to remove all information except for the choice of signs. This is similar to how spoken language text makes speech anonymous to the degree of word choice. Practically, for anonymizing sign language videos, we propose the combination of sign language segmentation (Moryossef et al., 2023a) with phonological sign language transcription. The bottleneck that transcribed sign segments introduce guarantees the removal of identifying information such as appearance, prosodic cues, and movement patterns. Then, a sign language synthesis component should synthesize the transcribed signing sequence back into video.

One major limitation of our study is the lack of human evaluation. While the method aims to preserve essential signing information, it's crucial to assess whether altering the signer's appearance affects the naturalness and comprehensibility of the signs for human viewers, especially in real-world contexts. Evaluating whether the anonymized or transferred appearances still allow viewers to recognize or identify individual signers is key to ensuring the method's success in obfuscating identity. This evaluation will provide insight into how well the technique balances privacy with the utility and intelligibility of the sign content.

Acknowledgements

This work was funded by the SIGMA project (G-95017-01-07) at the Digital Society Initiative (DSI), University of Zurich, and by `sign.mt` ltd.

References

Alessia Battisti, Emma van den Bold, Anne Göhring, Franz Holzknecht, and Sarah Ebling. 2024. Person identification from pose estimates in sign language. In *Proceedings of the LREC-COLING 2024 11th Workshop on the Representation and Processing of Sign Languages: Evaluation of Sign Language Resources*, pages 13–25, Torino, Italia. ELRA and ICCL.

Danielle Bragg, Oscar Koller, Naomi Caselli, and William Thies. 2020. Exploring collection of sign language datasets: Privacy, participation, and model performance. In *Proceedings of the 22nd International ACM SIGACCESS Conference on Computers and Accessibility*, ASSETS '20, New York, NY, USA. Association for Computing Machinery.

European Parliament and Council of the European Union. 2016. Regulation (EU) 2016/679 of the European Parliament and of the Council.

Ian Goodfellow, Jean Pouget-Abadie, Mehdi Mirza, Bing Xu, David Warde-Farley, Sherjil Ozair, Aaron Courville, and Yoshua Bengio. 2014. Generative adversarial nets. In *Advances in Neural Information Processing Systems*, volume 27. Curran Associates, Inc.

Thomas Hanke, Marc Schulder, Reiner Konrad, and Elena Jahn. 2020. Extending the Public DGS Corpus in size and depth. In *Proceedings of the LREC2020 9th Workshop on the Representation and Processing of Sign Languages: Sign Language Resources in the Service of the Language Community, Technological Challenges and Application Perspectives*, pages 75–82, Marseille, France. European Language Resources Association (ELRA).

Amy Isard. 2020. Approaches to the anonymisation of sign language corpora. In *SIGNLANG*.

Amit Moryossef, Zifan Jiang, Mathias Müller, Sarah Ebling, and Yoav Goldberg. 2023a. Linguistically motivated sign language segmentation. In *Findings of the Association for Computational Linguistics: EMNLP 2023*, pages 12703–12724, Singapore. Association for Computational Linguistics.

Amit Moryossef, Mathias Müller, and Rebecka Fahrni. 2021a. pose-format: Library for viewing, augmenting, and handling .pose files. `https://github.com/sign-language-processing/pose`.

Amit Moryossef, Mathias Müller, Anne Göhring, Zifan Jiang, Yoav Goldberg, and Sarah Ebling. 2023b. An open-source gloss-based baseline for spoken to signed language translation. In *2nd International Workshop on Automatic Translation for Signed and Spoken Languages (AT4SSL)*. Available at: `https://arxiv.org/abs/2305.17714`.

Amit Moryossef, Ioannis Tsochantaridis, Joe Dinn, Necati Cihan Camgöz, Richard Bowden, Tao Jiang, Annette Rios, Mathias Müller, and Sarah Ebling. 2021b. Evaluating the immediate applicability of pose estimation for sign language recognition. In *2021 IEEE/CVF Conference on Computer Vision and Pattern Recognition Workshops (CVPRW)*, pages 3429–3435.

Robin Rombach, Andreas Blattmann, Dominik Lorenz, Patrick Esser, and Björn Ommer. 2021. High-resolution image synthesis with latent diffusion models.

Phillip Rust, Bowen Shi, Skyler Wang, Necati Cihan Camgoz, and Jean Maillard. 2024. Towards privacy-aware sign language translation at scale. In *Annual Meeting of the Association for Computational Linguistics*.

Gerard Sant and Carlos Escolano. 2023. Analysis of acoustic information in end-to-end spoken language translation. In *INTERSPEECH 2023*, pages 52–56.

Ben Saunders, Necati Cihan Camgöz, and Richard Bowden. 2021. Anonysign: Novel human appearance synthesis for sign language video anonymisation. In *2021 16th IEEE International Conference on Automatic Face and Gesture Recognition (FG 2021)*, pages 1–8.

Ozge Mercanoglu Sincan and Hacer Yalim Keles. 2020. Autsl: A large scale multi-modal turkish sign language dataset and baseline methods. *IEEE Access*, 8:181340–181355.

Christina O. Tze, Panagiotis P. Filntisis, Anastasios Roussos, and Petros Maragos. 2022. Cartoonized anonymization of sign language videos. In *2022 IEEE 14th Image, Video, and Multidimensional Signal Processing Workshop (IVMSP)*, pages 1–5.

Lvmin Zhang and Maneesh Agrawala. 2023. Adding conditional control to text-to-image diffusion models.

Spontaneous Catalan Sign Language Recognition: Data Acquisition and Classification

Naiara Garmendia and **Horacio Saggion** and **Euan McGill**
TALN Natural Language Processing Group
Department of Engineering / Universitat Pompeu Fabra
C/Tànger 122
Barcelona, Spain (08018)

Abstract

This work presents the first investigation into Spontaneous Isolated Sign Language Recognition for Catalan Sign Language (LSC). Our work is grounded on the derivation of a dataset of signs and their glosses from a corpus of spontaneous dialogues and monologues. The recognition model is based on a Multi-Scale Graph Convolutional network fitted to our data. Results are promising since several signs are recognized with a high level of accuracy, and an average accuracy of 71% on the top 5 predicted classes from a total of 105 available. An interactive interface with experimental results is also presented. The data and software are made available to the research community.

1 Introduction

There remains a barrier of accessibility to information for communities of low-resource languages, and this is particularly acute for Sign Language (SL) users. The World Federation of the Deaf reported that there are approximately 70 million deaf people (Sign.mt Project, 2023) for many of whom SL is their main communication means, many of whom would benefit from being able to access public information, education, and media through a given SL.

Several natural language applications such as speech recognition or machine translation are at an advanced stage of development, thanks state of the art machine learning methods. Sign Language Technology research aims to develop usable technology with the deaf community in to aid communication and accessibility.

This type of research has been demonstrated by recent EU projects such as EASIER (Fox et al., 2025) and SignON (Vandeghinste et al., 2023). However, the provision of technology for sign languages remains a hard nut to crack due to several factors including the limited number of available corpora to train SL applications (De Sisto et al., 2022), the small size of these resources, and the multimodal characteristics of SLs.

SLs are the primary method of communication for deaf and hard-of-hearing (DHH) people. They are produced in the visual-spatial modality (rather than the oral-auditory modality of spoken languages) using manual articulators (the hands), and non-manual articulators such as facial expression, eye gaze and the physical space on and around the signer. SLs have structure and complexity comparable to spoken languages with rules and grammars ruling the way in which signs are formed and sequenced. They also undergo similar phenomena to spoken languages, including sociolinguistic variation (Lucas and Bayley, 2016), language acquisition patterns and psycholinguistic encoding (Baker et al., 2016).

Sign language processing (Yin et al., 2021) aims to uncover linguistic structures from a multimodal stream of information. There is added complexity in that signs may be produced simultaneously, i.e. one on each hand. This fact means that SL tools must also tackle simultaneity of input from multiple information streams. The field of SL processing has long been the concern of computer vision (CV) research sometimes without involvement of NLP: Tasks such as SL detection (Borg and Camilleri, 2019), identification (Monteiro et al., 2016) and segmentation (Renz et al., 2021) have all been addressed within a CV paradigm.

In this paper we are concerned with the development of technology for the recognition and classification of "spontaneous" signs extracted from conversations or monologues. This is a challenging endeavour when compared to the recognition of non-spontaneous isolated signs (Núñez-Marcos et al., 2023). Here we address this challenge for

Proceedings of the Third International Workshop on Automatic Translation for Signed and Spoken Languages (AT4SSL), pages 7–15, June 24, 2025

Catalan Sign Language[1] or LSC which has, to be best of our knowledge, never been addressed before in this context.

The two main contributions of this paper are as follows[2]:

- The creation of the first dataset of isolated signs derived from an available LSC corpus of continuous signing.
- The first exploratory Machine Learning based computer vision experiments on the LSC Corpus showing the promises and challenges of the task.

The rest of the paper is organized as follows: In the next Section we describe work related to Sign Language recognition with an emphasis on the approaches on which this work is based. Then, in Section 3 we briefly describe Catalan Sign Language and the dataset used in our experiments. In Section 4 we describe the methodology, including aspects related to the data processing and a description of our interface. This interface allows a user to explore the extracted data by searching by sign name (i.e., gloss). Then, in Section 5 we report experimental results and analysis. In Section 6 we discuss limitations and ethical considerations of our approach, finally closing the paper in Section 7 with a conclusion.

2 Related Work

Sign Language recognition (SLR) has made marked progress in recent years (Rastgoo et al., 2021; Núñez-Marcos et al., 2023). Continuous work on creating and collecting new datasets, including both isolated signs and continuous sign language, has greatly contributed to this advancement (Albanie et al., 2021; Duarte et al., 2021; Forster et al., 2014). These datasets provide essential resources for training SLR systems, and improving their robustness and accuracy. To process and analyse these signs effectively, different deep learning models are applied such as transformers (Camgöz et al., 2020; Liu et al., 2023) or LSTMs (Buttar et al., 2023). One important contribution introduces the Word-Level American Sign Language (WLASL) dataset (Li et al., 2020). This dataset is comprised of over 21,000 video samples of 2,000 American Sign Language (ASL) signs performed by more than 100 signers, making it one of the largest publicly available resources for word-level ASL recognition. The study evaluates various deep learning methods, including holistic visual appearance-based models (Rasiwasia and Vasconcelos, 2012) and 2D human pose-based methods. Among the evaluated models, the Inflated 3D ConvNet (I3D) achieves the highest performance. In the WLASL dataset with 300 classes, it reaches a top-1 accuracy of 56.14% and a top-5 accuracy of 79.94%. When scaled to 2,000 classes the performance decreases, obtaining a top-1 accuracy of 32.48% and a top-5 accuracy of 57.31%. Similarly, ASL Citizen (Desai et al., 2023b) is a large-scale dataset consisting of 83,399 videos covering 2,731 isolated signs performed by 52 signers. However, a key distinction is that ASL Citizen is built through a community-based crowd-sourcing approach (Bragg et al., 2022), allowing for a more diverse range of signing styles, environmental conditions, and recording setups. Our work is closely related to research on Spanish Sign Language (LSE) recognition (Vázquez-Enríquez et al., 2024). This work created a dataset – SWL-LSE – consisting of 8,000 instances of 300 isolated signs related to health, elicited from 124 participants through an online application. The signs were annotated using key points extracted with MediaPipe Holistic (Lugaresi et al., 2019). SWL-LSE specifically targets LSE and a health-related vocabulary, providing a domain-specific resource for improving accessibility in medical contexts. Additionally, this work has improved upon previous models by utilizing the Multi-Scale Graph Convolutional Network (MSG3D) instead of I3D, demonstrating enhanced performance in recognizing sign language glosses. It achieves a maximum accuracy of 92.83% without pre-training, which improved to 94.50% with ASL Citizen pre-training. Building upon these works, our research focuses on extracting gloss annotated signs from spontaneous LSC and classifying them using MSG3D. Using the strengths of existing datasets and methodologies, we aim to enhance the recognition of spontaneous LSC signs.

3 Catalan Sign Language

According to Romano (2016), Catalan Sign Language is used by approximately 30,000 people.

[1]Llengua de signes catalana.

[2]The data and software produced in this research can be found in Github (https://github.com/LaSTUS-TALN-UPF/Spontaneous-LSC-Recognition) and soon to be incorporated into the main LSC Corpus (https://lsc.iec.cat/en/1214/).

LSC is an official language recognized by the Catalan government with a first grammar published relatively early (Quer et al., 2005) and recently extended in Quer et al. (2020). LSC is legally[3] recognized which enables its use as a means of communication, learning, teaching and information access.

With regards to its origins, it is likely in the Francosign family (Quer, 2012; Hammarström et al., 2024), meaning that it shares some features with ASL and many European SLs. Like other SLs, LSC fulfils all possible communicative functions and, like any living language, has characteristics that distinguish it. LSC has evolved since its beginnings and continues to evolve through its interaction with other signed and spoken languages.

3.1 Annotation

There are various notation systems for SLs, ranging from phonemic transcription methods to a more abstract semi-phonemic alphabets to capture signs. Examples include SignWriting image-like representation[4], HamNoSys (Hanke, 2004) - a universal system based on the linear annotation of signs based on hand shape, hand location and movement - or the Stokoe notation (Stokoe et al., 1965) for ASL - composed of information on location, hand-shape, movement, and orientation. However, these writing systems are not used in a standardised way across datasets and studies, nor are they widely known by signers themselves. SL writing systems tend to be cumbersome to use and complex. In addition, signers tend to use writing systems based on a spoken language when it is necessary to communicate through text (Jantunen et al., 2021).

Glosses, a lexeme-based representation of a sign, are a commonly used system to transcribe SL into the ambient hearing society language where the SL is used - such as English in the United States, where ASL is mainly used or Spanish for LSE. There are many well-established issues with glossing, such as its inability to capture the full representation of a sign (e.g. movement in space), or a suitably rich semantic representation (Núñez-Marcos et al., 2023). Moreover, in order to gloss a stream of signs, a standard well-established gloss lexicon or dictionary is needed, which is, for the time being, not available for most SLs. However, the dataset we rely on provides rich gloss annotations that we use for sign classification. The data is annotated following the ELAN file specification (Max Planck Institute for Psycholinguistics, 2024; Wittenburg et al., 2006).

3.2 Corpus

The Catalan Sign Language (LSC) Corpus (Institut d' Estudis Catalans, 2025) project was initiated in 2012 with the goal of creating a comprehensive reference resource. The project aimed to collect video recordings from a number of elicitation tasks as well as free conversation. They aim to capture the linguistic diversity of LSC, considering variation based on the age and geographical background of the signers.

Data in this corpus is stored and presented in the format found in signbanks (Cassidy et al., 2018). One of the key strengths of this dataset is that the videos have been manually annotated with glosses using an ELAN application (Wittenburg et al., 2006). These annotations provide the lexical diversity and linguistic richness of LSC, making the corpus an essential resource for research and sign language processing.

4 Methodology

4.1 Sign Extraction

To obtain isolated signs, each video was processed using its corresponding annotations in ELAN software (Wittenburg et al., 2006). This allows for precise marking of the each sign's start and end points. Through this method, individual signs were extracted and subsequently analysed. Since the representation of a gloss can vary depending on factors such as sentence structure, context, or discourse (De Sisto et al., 2022), each extracted instance requires careful examination to ensure accurate classification (see Figure 1).

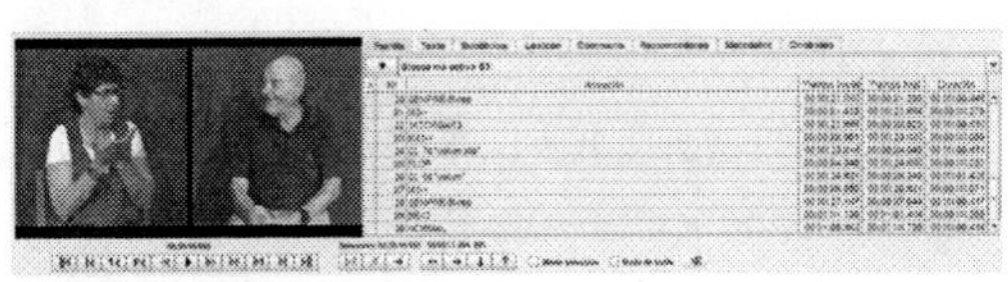

Figure 1: The ELAN application,with each gloss annotated with the precise time.

Unlike the previously mentioned datasets, where signers face the camera directly and produce each gloss in isolation, this dataset originates from continuous conversations. As a result, the camera

[3]See LLEI 17/2010, del 3 de juny, de la llengua de signes catalana: https://portaljuridic.gencat.cat/eli/es-ct/l/2010/06/03/17

[4]https://www.signwriting.org/archive/docs9/sw0821_SignWriting_Basics_Instruction_Manual_Sutton.pdf

angles are not always frontal, and sign production may be influenced by preceding or subsequent signs within the discourse. This introduces additional complexity, as the natural flow of conversation can affect the articulation and visual features of each sign, making their extraction and classification more challenging compared to datasets containing strictly isolated signs.

A total of 45,587 videos corresponding to 6,527 different glosses were collected. This large number of videos is due to the fact that glosses used to identify the signs are distinguished not only by their base form (e.g. lemma) but also by their variations in conjugation, phonological specification, among other factors.

As shown in Figure 2, the same gloss can appear with different specifications, such as hand position or the context in which it is used. By grouping all the variations of the same gloss, 1,885 main classes can be defined. In previous SL translation studies, a similar grouping is performed during preprocessing. Gloss variants only tend to be retained for different senses (Östling et al., 2017; McGill et al., 2024).

To analyze the variation in gloss representations, it was necessary to examine how frequently different forms of the same gloss appear in the dataset. The initial results indicate that many glosses appear with only a single variation. However, this is largely due to the fact that some glosses inherently have only one possible representation. To obtain a more realistic measure for this analysis, only glosses with more than 50 video samples were considered.

As shown in Figure 3, most glosses exhibit between three and 15 variations, with each variation typically represented by six to eight video samples. However, certain glosses display a much higher degree of variability. For instance, the gloss VEURE[5] appears in 74 different forms, while DONAR[6] has 49 variations. These cases suggest that some signs, particularly those frequently used in continuous signing, are more susceptible to variation. This could be influenced by factors such as coarticulation effects, signer-specific differences, or contextual adaptations within spontaneous communication.

The number of videos per gloss is not uniform, as some signs appear more frequently in conversa-

[5]'To see.'

[6]'To give.'

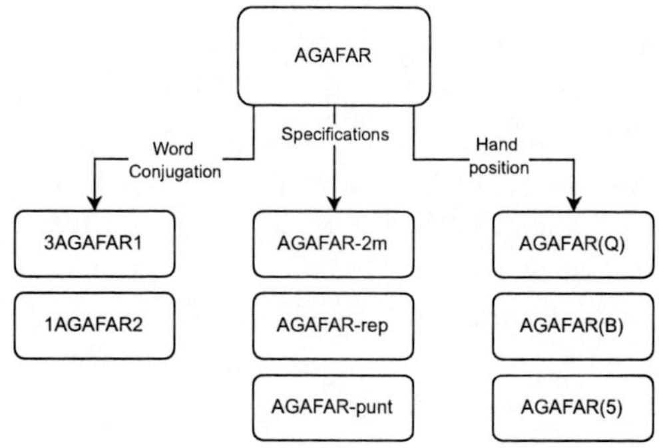

Figure 2: Variations of the sign agafar (i.e. *to take*): Subject/Object variation (e.g., grammatical person), Specifications (e.g. repetition), and hand configuration.

tions due to their recurrent use in the corpus (e.g. pronouns). Most glosses have between one and three variations, which is an insufficient amount to consider the sign well-defined or to provide enough data for a model to be properly learned. Due to this limitation, only glosses with more than 50 video instances were selected for further recognition tasks. This threshold was established based on the number of videos used in the previous studies. In Figure 4, it can be observed that the number of glosses with a large number of videos has a skewed distribution.

4.2 Sign Processing

Once the signs (and glosses) are extracted, pose estimation and keypoint detection are applied to analyse their movement and structure. This process is performed using MediaPipe (Lugaresi et al., 2019), which detects key body landmarks, including hand positions and body posture, from video data. Depending on project requirements, different keypoint sets can be extracted, including hands, body, and facial features.

These keypoints are then processed and transformed into a format suitable for model training and analysis. Additionally, derived features such as joint angles, bones, and movement patterns are computed, creating a structured dataset for tasks like gesture recognition and motion analysis. The visual example of a representation of that dataset is shown in Figure 5.

4.3 Interface

To facilitate the visualization of LSC Corpus Sign videos (the complete dialogues and monologues can be accessed through the LSC Corpus itself), an interface has been developed (see Figure 6).

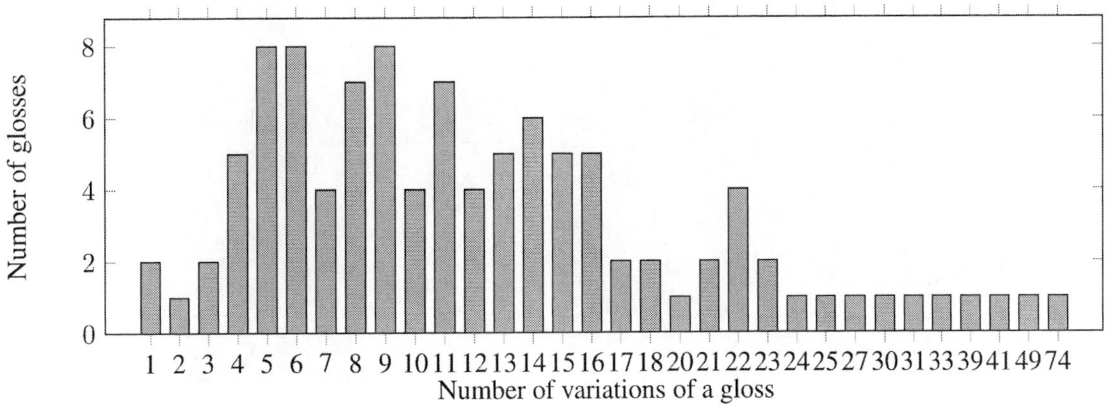

Figure 3: Analysis of 105 glosses and their variations

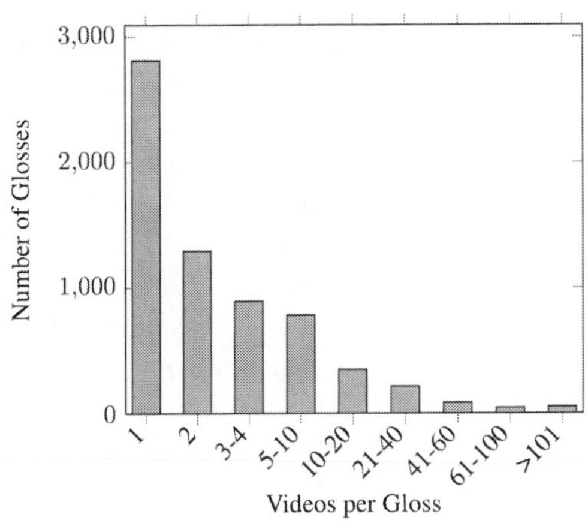

Figure 4: Number of videos per gloss

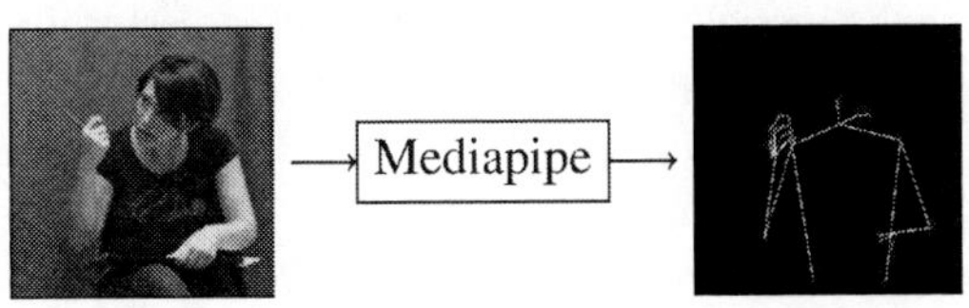

Figure 5: A pose estimation from MediaPipe from a video frame.

This interface allows users to view the segmented glosses, which are organized by gloss lemma (e.g. AGAFAR[7]). Additionally, for each video, the corresponding pose estimation extracted using MediaPipe is available. This tool provides a structured and interactive way to explore the dataset, ensuring accessibility to both the raw video data and the extracted motion features. This code is available on GitHub [8]. In addition, these tools will be integrated into the main LSC Corpus [9] space in the near future.

5 Experiments and Results

A model was trained using the code provided in the SWL-LSE study[10] (Vázquez-Enríquez et al., 2024), adapting it to the specific characteristics of this dataset. In this study, the MSG3D (Multi-Scale Graph Convolutional 3D) (Liu et al., 2020) model is used. This model operates on skeletal keypoints, making it particularly suited to ISLR. It utilizes Graph Convolution Networks (GCNs) to model spatial and temporal relationships between joints, capturing hand movements and body dynamics.

Since the data was extracted from continuous conversations, instances of the same sign can appear in varied forms. Some may be conjugated differently depending on the phrase and referent structure, while others may show variations in hand positioning between different signers.

To address these challenges, the dataset was organized into 105 classes. The objective is to train the model to recognize glosses regardless of these variations (i.e. "AGAFAR" instead of "3AGAFAR1", "AGAFAR-2n", etc. as seen in Figure 2), focusing on identifying the intended gloss lemma rather than its specific articulation in a given context. Hypothesizing that variations could be identified when context is made available to the model, we leave the identification of variations to future work.

The dataset consists of 15,000 video samples classified into 105 different classes, divided into training, validation, and test sets following a 70-15-15% split. Initially, the model was trained

[7] 'To take, to catch, to grasp.'

[8] https://github.com/LaSTUS-TALN-UPF/Spontaneous-LSC-Recognition

[9] https://lsc.iec.cat/en/1214/

[10] https://github.com/mvazquezgts/SWL-LSE

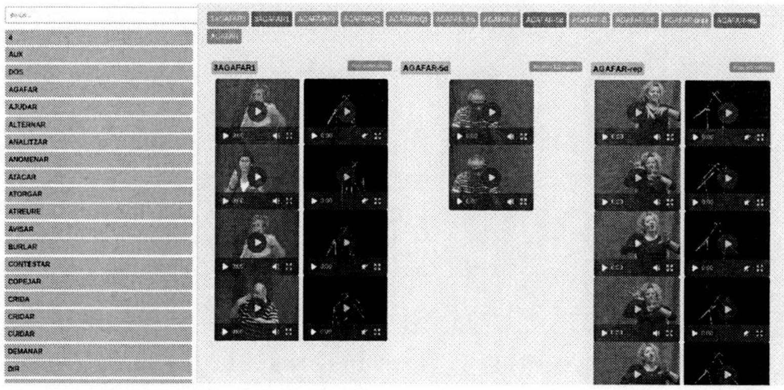

Figure 6: Screenshot of the interface, of the 'AGAFAR' (i.e., *to take or grasp*) page.

from scratch using only this dataset (*From Scratch* configuration). However, to assess whether pre-training could improve performance, additional experiments were conducted using pre-trained models on datasets such as SWL-LSE and ASL Citizen (Desai et al., 2023a) (*Pre-trained* configuration).

5.1 Experimental Configurations

Various hyperparameter configurations were explored to optimize the training process. The final selection was based on empirical results and best practices in action recognition.

- Optimizer: Stochastic Gradient Descent (SGD) with Nesterov momentum.
- Learning Rate & Scheduler: The initial learning rate was set to 0.01, with a ReduceLROnPlateau scheduler that adaptively reduces the learning rate by a factor of 0.5 when no improvement is observed for 10 epochs.
- Batch Size: A batch size of 16 was used for training, validation, and testing, which corresponds to the maximum capacity of the available GPU memory.
- Number of Epochs & Early Stopping: The model was trained for a maximum of 250 epochs, with early stopping applied if no improvement was observed for 30 consecutive epochs, thereby preventing overfitting and reducing computational costs.

5.2 Results and Analysis

The headline results of these experiments, comparing training form scratch versus pre-training on external datasets, are shown in Table 1. These results indicate that pre-training on the SWL-LSE dataset improves the model's ability to recognize signs. The Top-1 accuracy increased by 6.61%, while the Top-5 accuracy improved by 4.62%. This suggests that pre-training allows the model to generalize better, leveraging learned representations from a similar sign language dataset. To better understand where the model performs well and where it struggles, the accuracy per class was calculated. This analysis provides the strengths and weaknesses of the model's recognition capability. As shown in the Figure 7 the top 10 best-recognized signs achieved good accuracy: Between 72.5% and 90%, indicating that these signs are well-distinguished by the model. On the other hand, there are signs that show substantially lower accuracy with some of them featuring less than 10% accuracy. To further analyze the model's limitations, the lowest performing results were examined. The low accuracy of 'COM' (i.e. *as*), for example, can be attributed to its dependency on sentence context, as its articulation varies greatly based on preceding and following signs, making the sign articulation different depending on the context. In the case of 'SI' (i.e., *affirmation*), although the facial expressions clearly indicates affirmation, the variation in hand movement makes it difficult for the model to recognize it. This is due to the model primarily relying on hand motion.

6 Limitations and Ethics

Data limitation is evident for the experiments reported in this paper. The fact that conversations and monologues were elicited by prompting the signers on specific topics constrains the lexical diversity of the discourses, and therefore limiting the scope of the sign recognition system. Moreover, task type may also limit the variety of syntactic structures in the utterances and the signs within

Configuration	Top-1 Accuracy	Top-5 Accuracy
Scratch	42.63%	67.65%
Pre-trained (SWL)	49.24%	72.27%

Table 1: Results of the MSG3D model trained from sratch or from a pre-trained.

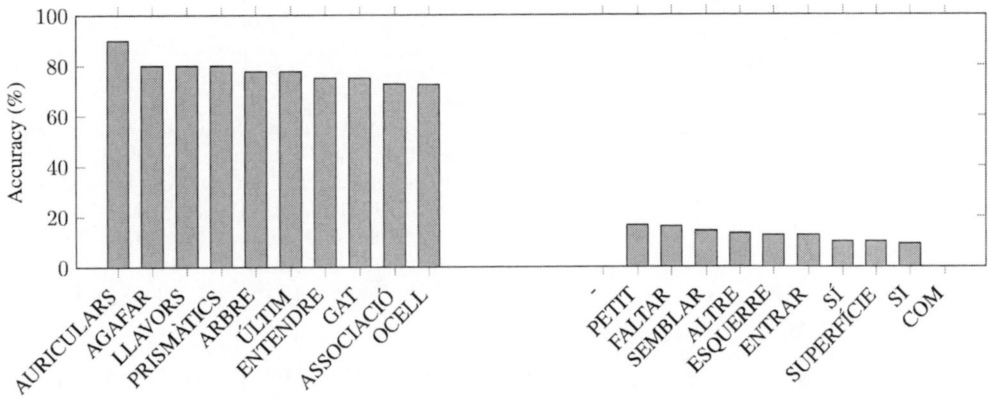

Figure 7: Best and Worst top-10 accuracies

them. Note, however, that several datasets for the study of SL linguistics have adopted similar data gathering methodologies (Shterionov et al., 2024). Only looking at the spans of the produced sign is a key limitation of the approach, since it does not allow the proposed method to use left and right context for a better-informed prediction. We will address this in future work by considering frames to the left and right of the actual sign. In relation to ethics, SL data in videos carry personal information which can lead to the identification of the signer, therefore specific care should be taken when manipulating the data. The corpus we have used is licenced under Creative Commons (CC BY 4.0) which allows the present work to be shared and adapted. It is worth noting that the dataset features native signers following recommendations for sign language research (Leeson et al., 2024).

7 Conclusion and Future Work

Providing language technology for sign languages contributes to a more inclusive and accessible society in compliance with the United Nations Human Rights Council.

In this paper we have presented the creation of a new dataset of spontaneous Signs in Catalan Sign Language, derived from a Corpus of spontaneous dialogues and monologues. We have carried out the first experiments on sign language recognition which achieved positive results when considering the challenging (i.e., spontaneous extracted from continuous signing) characteristics of the data when compared to other elicited datasets (i.e., non-spontaneous generated in isolation). We have tested two contemporary approaches to the task showing that by pre-training the models with diverse sign language data has a positive impact in recognition performance.

There are however many areas to explore in this field: (i) we plan to address the problem of sign segmentation from conversations, (ii) perform continuous sign language recognition over conversations, and (iii) develop translation technology to translate the output into Catalan language.

Acknowledgments

We are grateful to the reviewers for their useful comments which contributed to improvement of the present work. We would like to thank specially José Luis Alba Castro from Universidade de Vigo for useful discussions which helped ground the current work. We are indebted to Gemma Barberà and Josep Quer from Universitat Pompeu Fabra for sharing a version of the Catalan Sign Language corpus before its official release which helped jump-start our project. Finally, we acknowledge support from the Spanish State Research Agency under the Maria de Maeztu Units of Excellence Programme (CEX2021-001195-M).

References

Samuel Albanie, Gül Varol, Liliane Momeni, Hannah Bull, Triantafyllos Afouras, Himel Chowdhury, Neil Fox, Bencie Woll, Rob Cooper, Andrew McParland, and Andrew Zisserman. 2021. Bbc-oxford british sign language dataset. *Preprint*, arXiv:2111.03635.

A. E. Baker, Beppie van den Bogaerde, Roland Pfau, and Trude M. Schermer. 2016. *The linguistics of sign languages - an introduction.*

Mark Borg and Kenneth P. Camilleri. 2019. Sign Language Detection "in the Wild" with Recurrent Neural Networks. *ICASSP 2019 - 2019 IEEE International Conference on Acoustics, Speech and Signal Processing (ICASSP)*, pages 1637–1641.

Danielle Bragg, Abraham Glasser, Fyodor Minakov, Naomi Caselli, and William Thies. 2022. Exploring collection of sign language videos through crowdsourcing. *Proc. ACM Hum.-Comput. Interact.*, 6(CSCW2).

Ahmed Mateen Buttar, Usama Ahmad, Abdu H. Gumaei, Adel Assiri, Muhammad Azeem Akbar, and Bader Fahad Alkhamees. 2023. Deep learning in sign language recognition: A hybrid approach for the recognition of static and dynamic signs. *Mathematics*, 11(17).

Necati Cihan Camgöz, Oscar Koller, Simon Hadfield, and Richard Bowden. 2020. Sign language transformers: Joint end-to-end sign language recognition and translation. In *CVPR 2020*, pages 10020–10030.

Steve Cassidy, Onno Crasborn, Henri Nieminen, Wessel Stoop, Micha Hulsbosch, Susan Even, Erwin Komen, and Trevor Johnston. 2018. Signbank: Software to support web based dictionaries of sign language. In *Proceedings of the Eleventh International Conference on Language Resources and Evaluation (LREC 2018)*, Miyazaki, Japan. European Language Resources Association (ELRA).

Mirella De Sisto, Vincent Vandeghinste, Santiago Egea Gómez, Mathieu De Coster, Dimitar Shterionov, and Horacio Saggion. 2022. Challenges with sign language datasets for sign language recognition and translation. In *Proceedings of the Thirteenth Language Resources and Evaluation Conference*, pages 2478–2487, Marseille, France. European Language Resources Association.

Aashaka Desai, Lauren Berger, Fyodor O Minakov, Vanessa Milan, Chinmay Singh, Kriston Pumphrey, Richard E Ladner, Hal Daumé III, Alex X Lu, Naomi Caselli, and Danielle Bragg. 2023a. Asl citizen: A community-sourced dataset for advancing isolated sign language recognition. *arXiv preprint arXiv:2304.05934*.

Aashaka Desai, Lauren Berger, Fyodor O. Minakov, Vanessa Milan, Chinmay Singh, Kriston Pumphrey, Richard E. Ladner, Hal Daumé III, Alex X. Lu, Naomi Caselli, and Danielle Bragg. 2023b. Asl citizen: A community-sourced dataset for advancing isolated sign language recognition. *Preprint*, arXiv:2304.05934.

Amanda Duarte, Shruti Palaskar, Lucas Ventura, Deepti Ghadiyaram, Kenneth DeHaan, Florian Metze, Jordi Torres, and Xavier Giro-i Nieto. 2021. How2Sign: A Large-scale Multimodal Dataset for Continuous American Sign Language. In *Conference on Computer Vision and Pattern Recognition (CVPR)*.

Jens Forster, Christoph Schmidt, Oscar Koller, Martin Bellgardt, and Hermann Ney. 2014. Extensions of the sign language recognition and translation corpus RWTH-PHOENIX-weather. In *Proceedings of the Ninth International Conference on Language Resources and Evaluation (LREC'14)*, pages 1911–1916, Reykjavik, Iceland. European Language Resources Association (ELRA).

Neil Fox, Bencie Woll, and Kearsy Cormier. 2025. Best practices for sign language technology research. *Universal Access in the Information Society*, 24(1):69–77.

Harald Hammarström, Robert Forkel, Martin Haspelmath, and Sebastian Bank. 2024. Glottolog 5.0.

Thomas Hanke. 2004. Hamnosys—representing sign language data in language resources and language processing contexts. In *LREC 2004, WS on RPSLs*, pages 1–6, Paris, France.

Institut d' Estudis Catalans. 2025. Corpus de referència de la llengua de signes catalana (LSC) (CORPUS LSC). `https://corpuslsc.iec.cat/`.

Tommi Jantunen, Rebekah Rousi, Päivi Raino, Markku Turunen, Mohammad Valipoor, and Narciso García. 2021. *Is There Any Hope for Developing Automated Translation Technology for Sign Languages?*, pages 61–73.

Lorraine Leeson, Sara Morrissey, Dimitar Shterionov, Daniel Stein, Henk van den Heuvel, and Andy Way. 2024. How It Started and How It's Going: Sign Language Machine Translation and Engagement with Deaf Communities Over the Past 25 Years. In Andy Way, Lorraine Leeson, and Dimitar Shterionov, editors, *Sign Language Machine Translation*, pages 27–72. Springer Nature Switzerland, Cham.

Dongxu Li, Cristian Rodriguez Opazo, Xin Yu, and Hongdong Li. 2020. Word-level deep sign language recognition from video: A new large-scale dataset and methods comparison. *Preprint*, arXiv:1910.11006.

Yu Liu, Parma Nand, Md Akbar Hossain, Minh Nguyen, and Wei Qi Yan. 2023. Sign language recognition from digital videos using feature pyramid network with detection transformer.

Ziyu Liu, Hongwen Zhang, Zhenghao Chen, Zhiyong Wang, and Wanli Ouyang. 2020. Disentangling and unifying graph convolutions for skeleton-based action recognition. In *Proceedings of the IEEE/CVF Conference on Computer Vision and Pattern Recognition*, pages 143–152.

Ceil Lucas and Robert Bayley. 2016. Quantative sociolinguistics and sign languages: Implications for sociolinguistic theory. In Nikolas Coupland, editor, *Sociolinguistics: Theoretical Debates*, chapter 16, pages 349–366. Cambridge University Press, Cambridge, United Kingdom.

Camillo Lugaresi, Jiuqiang Tang, Hadon Nash, Chris McClanahan, Esha Uboweja, Michael Hays, Fan Zhang, Chuo-Ling Chang, Ming Guang Yong, Juhyun Lee, Wan-Teh Chang, Wei Hua, Manfred Georg, and Matthias Grundmann. 2019. Mediapipe: A framework for building perception pipelines. *Preprint*, arXiv:1906.08172.

Nijmegen The Netherlands Max Planck Institute for Psycholinguistics, The Language Archive. 2024. Elan (version 6.9) [computer software]. *Technologies*.

Euan McGill, Luis Chiruzzo, and Horacio Saggion. 2024. Bootstrapping pre-trained word embedding models for sign language gloss translation. In *Proceedings of the 25th Annual Conference of the European Association for Machine Translation (Volume 1)*, pages 116–132, Sheffield, UK. European Association for Machine Translation (EAMT).

Caio D. D. Monteiro, Christy Maria Mathew, Ricardo Gutierrez-Osuna, and Frank Shipman. 2016. Detecting and Identifying Sign Languages through Visual Features. In *2016 IEEE International Symposium on Multimedia (ISM)*, pages 287–290.

Adrián Núñez-Marcos, Olatz Perez de Viñaspre, and Gorka Labaka. 2023. A survey on sign language machine translation. *Expert Systems with Applications*, 213:118993.

Robert Östling, Carl Börstell, Moa Gärdenfors, and Mats Wirén. 2017. Universal dependencies for swedish sign language. In *Nordic Conference of Computational Linguistics*.

Josep Quer. 2012. Legal pathways to the recognition of sign languages: A comparison of the catalan and spanish sign language acts. *Sign Language Studies*, 12(4):565–582.

Josep Quer, Gemma Barberà Altimira, Gemma Barberà, Sara Cañas-Peña, Berta Moya-Avilés, Alexandra Navarrete-González, Raquel Veiga Busto, Aida Villaécija, and Giorgia Zorzi. 2020. *A Grammar of Catalan Sign Language (LSC)*. SIGN-HUB.

Josep Quer, Eva Ma. Rondoni, and Gemma. Barberà. 2005. Universitat de Barcelona, Barcelona.

Nikhil Rasiwasia and Nuno Vasconcelos. 2012. Holistic context models for visual recognition. *IEEE Transactions on Pattern Analysis and Machine Intelligence*, 34(5):902–917.

Razieh Rastgoo, Kourosh Kiani, and Sergio Escalera. 2021. Sign language recognition: A deep survey. *Expert Systems with Applications*, 164:113794.

Katrin Renz, Nicolaj C. Stache, Samuel Albanie, and Gül Varol. 2021. Sign Language Segmentation with Temporal Convolutional Networks. In *ICASSP*.

Isabel Romano. 2016. La llengua de signes catalana.

Dimitar Shterionov, Lorraine Leeson, and Andy Way. 2024. *The Pipeline of Sign Language Machine Translation*, pages 1–25. Springer Nature Switzerland, Cham.

Sign.mt Project. 2023. Sign language populations - sign.mt.

William Stokoe, Dorothy Casterline, and C. Croneberg. 1965. A Dictionary of American Sign Language on Linguistic Principles.

Vincent Vandeghinste, Dimitar Shterionov, Mirella De Sisto, Aoife Brady, Mathieu De Coster, Lorraine Leeson, Josep Blat, Frankie Picron, Marcello Paolo Scipioni, Aditya Parikh, Louis ten Bosch, John O'Flaherty, Joni Dambre, Jorn Rijckaert, Bram Vanroy, Victor Ubieto Nogales, Santiago Egea Gomez, Ineke Schuurman, Gorka Labaka, Adrián Núnez-Marcos, Irene Murtagh, Euan McGill, and Horacio Saggion. 2023. SignON: Sign language translation. progress and challenges. In *Proceedings of the 24th Annual Conference of the European Association for Machine Translation*, pages 501–502, Tampere, Finland. European Association for Machine Translation.

Manuel Vázquez-Enríquez, José Luis Alba-Castro, Laura Docío-Fernández, and Eduardo Rodríguez-Banga. 2024. Swl-lse: A dataset of health-related signs in spanish sign language with an islr baseline method. *Technologies*, 12(10).

Peter Wittenburg, Hennie Brugman, Albert Russel, Alex Klassmann, and Han Sloetjes. 2006. ELAN: a professional framework for multimodality research. In *Proceedings of the Fifth International Conference on Language Resources and Evaluation (LREC'06)*, Genoa, Italy. European Language Resources Association (ELRA).

Kayo Yin, Amit Moryossef, Julie Hochgesang, Yoav Goldberg, and Malihe Alikhani. 2021. Including Signed Languages in Natural Language Processing.

User Involvement in the Research and Development Life Cycle of Sign Language Machine Translation Systems

Lisa Lepp and **Dimitar Shterionov** and **Mirella De Sisto**
Department of Cognitive Science and Artificial Intelligence,
Tilburg University, 5037 AB Tilburg, The Netherlands

Abstract

Machine translation (MT) has evolved rapidly over the last 70 years, thanks to the advances in processing technology, methodologies, and the ever-increasing volumes of data. This trend is observed in the context of MT for spoken languages. However, when it comes to sign language (SL) translation technologies, the progress is much slower; sign language machine translation (SLMT) is still in its infancy with limited applications. One of the main factors for this set back is the lack of effective, respectful and fair user involvement across the different phases of the research and development of SLMT.

We present a meta-review of 111 articles on SLMT from the perspective of user involvement. Our analysis investigates which users are involved, and what tasks they assume in the first four phrases of MT research: (i) Problem and definition, (ii) Dataset construction, (iii) Model Design and Training, (iv) Model Validation and Evaluation. We find out that users have primarily been involved as data creators and monitors as well as evaluators. We assess that effective co-creation, as defined in (Lepp et al., 2025), has not been performed and conclude with recommendations for improving the MT research and development landscape from a co-creative perspective.

1 Introduction, Motivation and Related Work

Machine translation (MT) has evolved rapidly over the last 70 years. The first MT systems, i.e., rule-based MT, built around human-crafted rules and dictionaries, followed a very human-intensive process. With the shift towards data-driven MT, the MT development process became structured around the collection and processing of large volumes of data with the use of powerful computational tools. This process was distributed over distinct human-intensive (e.g. data collection) as well as computationally-heavy tasks (e.g. training a word-alignment with a tool such as giza++ (Och and Ney, 2003) or training an encoder-decoder neural network (Bahdanau et al., 2015)), aiming to reduce human efforts in quickly delivering effective and efficient MT systems. Along the way, it aligned with the generic machine learning (ML) and deep learning (DL) practices, and as such can be divided into six key phases: (i) Problem and use-case definition and solution ideation, (ii) Dataset construction, (iii) Model development, (iv) Quality assessment (automatic and / or human), (v) Model deployment and (vi) Monitoring and maintenance.[1] In the context of MT, humans with different expertise are involved in these stages, e.g. native speakers generate new data; native speakers and professional translators evaluate MT output; linguists participate in the data processing and preparation; engineers and computer scientists develop model architectures and train models.

MT primarily addresses text-to-text, text-to-speech, and speech- to text use-cases, which pertain to Spoken Languages (SpLs), where substantial progress and qualities matching human standards are now observed. When it comes to user involvement in MT projects, users may take part in the data collection and in the evaluation stages, but are rarely involved in the other stages.

Translation technologies for SLs, however, have not progressed as quickly as SpL MT. Challenges related to data, modeling and the complexity of processing are significant contributors to this slow

[1]These phases or stages may vary depending on the granularity or the grouping of sub stages. E.g., another 5-phase formulation is: (i) Problem definition, (ii) Dataset collection and processing, (iii) Model Design and Training, (iv) Model Validation and Evaluation and (v) Model deployment and maintenance.

Proceedings of the Third International Workshop on Automatic Translation for Signed and Spoken Languages (AT4SSL), pages 16–36, June 24, 2025

progress. An equally important consideration is the role of humans. In SLMT and Natural Sign Language Processing (NSLP), SL data is typically collected in the form of video recordings of signing individuals. The typical SLMT process still involves distinct transformation phases (Shterionov et al., 2024), which require human intervention. In these fields, humans are crucial not just as data creators, evaluators, or monitors, but also as active partners in developing practical and socially impactful SLMT systems.

Caselli et al. (2021) acknowledge the need to better include users in the research process and advocate for a more user-involving natural language processing (NLP) research. They wrote 9 guidelines for participatory design in NLP (we summarize these in Appendix B). Harder et al. (2013) analyses user involvement in different fields and propose a participation typology which ranges over various degrees of user involvement. However, in the context of SpL MT and NLP research there are no clear indications for the increase in user-involvement over the whole life-cycle. As advocated by (Caselli et al., 2021), engaging user communities in NLP projects is essential. However, in this field, the term *co-creation* typically refers to human-AI collaboration for content generation, as explored in recent studies (Sharma et al., 2024; Konen et al., 2024; Ding et al., 2023) on optimizing interactions between large language models (LLMs) and human creators. Co-creative methods have also been applied to tasks like poetry generation (Gonçalo Oliveira et al., 2017), literature synthesis (Manjavacas et al., 2017), and interpreting (Nakaguchi et al., 2016), and there no significant work demonstrating effective user involvement for MT.[2] While this may not be significantly problematic for the adoption of translation technologies for SpLs at present,[3] it has a negative impact on SLMT research progress and adoption due to issues related to lack of expectation management through unacceptable and impractical outputs (e.g. SL translation gloves) to unethical research (e.g. involving non-signers in the data creation process). The recent work of Lepp et al. (2025) proposes a formal definition of co-creation for SLMT according to which users contribute as equal partners [4] in the SLMT project as well as a participatory typology to aid the assessment of SL user and SL community (SLC) members involvement in such projects. We must emphasize the following points. First, not every SL user is inherently part of a SLC. The term "SLC" may suggest that it encompasses all variations in SL fluency, equal access to a visual language, and educational opportunities, but this is not the case, as highlighted by the American National Association of the Deaf[5]. Therefore, we draw a clear distinction between SLCs and SL users, ensuring that SL users outside of an SLC — for example, Hard-of-Hearing (HoH) signing individuals[6]—are also acknowledged, along with individuals who are part of an SLC.[7]

Reflecting on co-creative and user-involving practices, they analyses 111 articles to identify the degree of involvement of SL users and SLC members. They use an adaptation of (Harder et al., 2013)'s typology for the specific case of SLMT and NSLP,[8]. Their analysis provides a generic overview of these articles. However, the necessity and feasibility of co-creation may differ significantly across the phases of the ML life cycle (or MT life cycle). For instance, dataset construction is an area where user involvement is often critical, while model design and training may present practical challenges in integrating co-creation effectively.

We take the work of (Lepp et al., 2025) one step further and conduct a deeper review of the 111 articles on SLMT based on (1) the involvement of the SL user per *research and development phase*, and (2) the roles of the involved SL user and / or

[2]An ACL Anthology search from Oct 7, 2024 found 146 relevant works overall.

[3]Current language technologies have evolved and spread to an extent that they have become indispensable part of professional and non-professional translation activities.

[4]With equal partners, we propose involving SL users and the SLC as essential collaborators during the MT phases.

[5]https://www.nad.org/resources/american-sign-language/community-and-culture-frequently-asked-questions/

[6]We drew the distinction between Hard of Hearing (HoH) and Deaf from the literature review in 2; however, this does not imply that HoH individuals are inherently less fluent in sign language than Deaf individuals. Fluency and authenticity in sign language are not determined by medical hearing status, but rather by individual preferences and choices in language use.

[7]Similar to SpLs, SLs are dynamic languages with dialects and regional variations, particularly in vocabulary. Furthermore, there are home-signs, family-signs, village-signs, and individual signs, among others. Most existing SLMT models, methods, and databases rely on standardized SL, which makes it challenging to accommodate these variations. Since we advocate for co-creation to leverage diverse perspectives, it is essential to consider these inter-signer variations when developing SLMT models, methods, and databases.

[8]We summarize their typology in Appendix A.

the kind of functions or task they have fulfilled (if can be derived from the reviewed article).

The granular assessment of user involvement we provide in this work, leads to better insights into where participation is needed and what efforts should be focused on better involving SL users and SLC members. We identify where and to what extent projects have been co-created and where there is room for improvement. Doing so, we contribute to the literature gap of to what extent the SLC has been involved throughout the different phases in the research life cycle of a technical project.

This paper is structured as follows: in Section 2 we provide our meta-review of the 111 articles referenced in (Núñez-Marcos et al., 2023; Coster et al., 2024). Next, we present with the assessment of user involvement per MT phase in Section 2.2. Section 3 presents a discussion and a critical reflection follows in Section 4. We conclude in Section 5 with general remarks and directions for future work.

2 Meta-review of user involvement and co-creation

In 2023 and 2024, two review articles of SLMT were published by Coster et al. (2024) and Núñez-Marcos et al. (2023). These articles contain an overview of a large volume of literature on SLMT, focusing on the technological solutions, different approaches and historical advancements. To the best of our knowledge, these are the most complete and recent historical overviews of work in the field of SLMT and NSLP. We conducted a meta-review, i.e., a manual analysis, of the SLMT-related papers reviewed in (Coster et al., 2024) and (Núñez-Marcos et al., 2023) from the perspective of (1) SL users involvement per ML research phase and (2) the roles that the SL users had in these phases. We rely on their work for our meta-review because in addition to their recency as literature review works our insights can directly complement their findings. That is, we believe our work fills in the societal gap of these works. We do acknowledge the fact that our work does not involve the articles beyond 2023 and we leave this for future work where a new study should look into both technological (theirs) as well societal (ours) aspect of SLMT and NSLP work.

2.1 Selection and filtering criteria

To align our analysis with the work of (Lepp et al., 2025), we follow their selection criteria. These are:

- The article needs to be mentioned in (Coster et al., 2024) or (Núñez-Marcos et al., 2023);
- The article needs to have open access;[9]
- The study should focus on SLMT, or on one of the phases;
- The study should focus on translation of SLs or between SLs and SpLs in either direction (but not only on SpLs);

After these exclusion steps, the remaining **111 articles**, (56,9 % of the original 193) were considered in the following discussion. For completeness, we list these 111 papers in Appendix C.[10]

2.2 User involvement in SLMT-research

To gain insights on the user involvement in the SLMT research and development projects covered by the aforementioned articles, we decompose these projects according to the typical machine learning (ML) phases most-commonly adopted in MT (noted in Section 1) – (i) Problem and use-case definition and solution ideation, (ii) Dataset construction, (iii) Model development, (iv) Quality assessment (automatic and / or human), (v) Model deployment and (vi) Monitoring and maintenance – and consider the first four phases. We did not look beyond the phase of quality assessment, i.e. Phase (iv), as the reviewed articles do not cover phases (v) and (vi). We categorize these papers according to the phases of the MT research life cycle to assess the extent of user involvement as a proxy to co-creation implementation and identify areas for improvement.

We also analyzed the kind of roles the SL user may have had, and —if it is clear– what kind of tasks they worked on during the different MT research life cycle phases.

Table 1 presents a summary of the overall distribution of articles—both with and without user involvement classified across the four different phases of the research life cycle in an MT project.

The results in Table 1 shows that the user has been involved in 11% of the reviewed articles across one of the research phases: less than 1% of the articles follow co-creation practices in phases

[9]As one of the reviewers rightly mentioned, some works were excluded that might have been more co-creation based. However, since we decided to align with (Lepp et al., 2025), we applied the same selection criteria.

[10]These are the same articles that are listed in the work of Lepp et al. (2025) but for completeness we add them to this paper.

(i) and (iii); 5% – in phase (ii) and 6.9% in phase (iv).

2.3 Roles, tasks and functions

As outlined in (Lepp et al., 2025), (Harder et al., 2013), and (Caselli et al., 2021), co-creation involves a diverse group of actors (users, researchers, etc.) with different roles. We further analyze the articles within the 11% in the "With user involvement" column in Table 1, which follow some form of co-creation. We examined who the user was carried out, the tasks assigned to the SL users (if specified), and in which phases they were involved. This data is presented in Table 2.

The roles and user types listed in Table 2 are presented as they appear in the reviewed articles. Although some of these roles might seem to fit together in one group, we maintain them separately due to the additional information or uncertainty they carry. For instance, "Deaf and Hearing" may or may not include team members, whereas "Deaf and Hearing team members" explicitly indicates that the individuals are part of the development team (as reflected in their assigned roles). Based on this, we offer the following general observations:

1. User types span over 24 different user type-role combinations. We distinguish 8 user types: Hearing, Deaf –across different regions–, HoH, CoDa[11], as well as Experts [12], Interpreters, Linguists, and Teachers (with or without an indication whether these are hearing, deaf or HoH individuals); and 4 tasks (which determine the role these individuals "play"): data recording, data annotation, data collection[13] and participating as a member of the research and development team. We recognize that row 6 (e.g., deaf experts in Table 2) is marked as 0, 0, 0, 0 for the analyzed phases. However, as noted by Coster et al. (2019), Desai et al. (2024), and Marshall and Sáfár (2002) that discusses the importance of 'co-creation with the DHH community' and 'the value of feedback and guidance from Deaf users', we have categorized this subgroup as 'Deaf experts'.

2. When comparing these roles with the advanced typology of relationships (see Appendix A from (Lepp et al., 2025)), we observe that there is a clear gap of engagement between researchers and SL users and/or SLCs. This aligns with Level -1 (Denigration –direct or indirect impact), Level 0 (Neglect) or Level 1 (Learning From). In the article of López-Ludeña et al. (2012), there is a combination of Deaf and Hearing participants. In another paper, that of Ebling and Huenerfauth (2015), both Deaf and Hearing team members were involved, but despite the promising nature of their involvement, it was limited to the data collection phase. We can state, based on these findings, that the researcher holds the *power*, particularly in phases (i) and (iii), and is the *sole decision-maker* throughout *all* phases of the MT project.

3. When comparing Table 2 with the guidelines from (Caselli et al., 2021), we observe that these distinct roles do not align with several of the guidelines: Principle 1 – there is no discussion leading to consensus; Principle 2 – the process is not reflexive but limited to one or two phrases; Principle 3 and Principle 4 – SL users are predetermined and treated as data; Principle 5 – wider communities are not involved, and Principle 7 – language has been seen as an end, rather than a means. Additionally, Principle 8 (consent versus intrusion) and Principle 9 (considering the dynamics) are debatable, as there is a lack of meta-data regarding the appropriateness of the involvement or the application for grants in these MT processes.

3 Discussion of user involvement per phase

We delve into these articles further and hints to several tendencies of positive and negative practices broken down per phase.

1. **Phase (i): Problem and use-case definition, and solution ideation**

[11] i.e. Children of Deaf Adults

[12] For the definition of *Expert*, we adopt the following description: an individual who possesses a comprehensive and profound understanding, along with competence in knowledge, skills, and experience, acquired through practice and education in a specific field or area of study `https://en.wikipedia.org/wiki/Expert?utm_source=chatgpt.com`

[13] We distinguish between data recording and data collection with the former involving the user in the recording of SL data, while the latter may imply that the user is tasked to collect existing (already recorded) data.

Research phases	No user involvement	User involvement
(i)Problem and definition	110	1
(ii)Data Construction	89	22
(iii)Model Design Training	110	1
(iv)Model Validation and Evaluation	94	17
Total	403	41

Table 1: The amount of reviewed articles per MT research phase over two categories: with or without user involvement.

	Phases				
Actor category and task	**(i)**	**(ii)**	**(iii)**	**(iv)**	**Total**
1. Hearing only	0	1	0	1	2
2. HoH only	0	1	0	0	1
3. Deaf only	0	2	1	5	8
4. CoDa only	0	0	0	0	0
5. Deaf and hearing	0	0	0	2	2
6. Deaf experts	0	0	0	0	0
7. Hearing and Deaf experts	0	1	0	0	1
8. Deaf signers across different regions	0	1	0	0	1
9. Deaf for data recordings	0	2	0	0	2
10. Deaf for data annotations	0	1	0	0	1
11. Deaf for data recordings and annotations	0	1	0	0	1
12. Deaf for data-collection	0	1	0	0	1
13. Deaf via Video-channel	0	1	0	0	1
14. Interpreters	0	1	0	1	2
15. Interpreters and CoDa's	0	1	0	0	1
16. Interpreters and Deaf	0	1	0	1	2
17. Deaf and Hearing team-members	0	1	0	0	1
18. Linguists	0	0	0	2	2
19. Teachers	0	1	0	1	2
20. Expertise unclear	1	0	0	2	3
21. Linguists and teachers	0	1	0	0	1
22. Teachers + Deaf across different regions	0	2	0	0	2
23. Deaf experts and interpreters	0	1	0	0	1
24. Deaf and CoDa for video recordings	0	1	0	0	1
Total:	1	22	1	17	41

Table 2: The amount of articles which include co-creative practices and the roles of participants they mention, categorized over the four research phases of MT.

There is only one article –i.e Morrissey and Way (2007), that notes involvement in phase (i). This observation contradicts Principles 1, 2, 6 and 9 of (Caselli et al., 2021). That is, in an effective co-creative project, users and developers should be in agreement early on of its development (Principle 1); as recommended in Principles 2 and 6, the design, which is encapsulated in phase (i) as well as in (iii), should be a continuous process; Principle 9 suggests the involvement of the users and the community at a stage where goals are discussed and decided, which, typically, takes place in phase (i) of an SLMT project.

2. **Phase (ii): Dataset construction** We observe that in the current MT landscape, as shown in Table 2, the SL user is primarily involved in data recording, data collection, or annotation tasks. This observation conflicts with

recommendations of the most relevant Principles of (Caselli et al., 2021) – Principle 7 (Language is a means rather than an end) and Principle 4 (Data and communities are not separate). Following the typology of Lepp et al. (2025), work that only includes SL users in data collection and processing tasks would be classified as Level 0 or Level 1. Furthermore, despite involvement of SL users in this phase (the largest number among all phases), there are considerations that need to be taken into account. These include what data will be created, who will create it, how many signers are involved, and whether they are representative of the population from which the data is gathered. For example, the work of Vandeghinste et al. (2024); Sisto et al. (2022); De Meulder (2021) differentiate between SL data as a source (original data) and SL data as a target (translated from SpL data), with the latter case potentially leading to MT producing less natural translations; their research also underlines that non-native signers produce SL data that is impacted by their first language. Another issue relate to the collection method and technical setup for best human-computer interaction. For example, Jedlička et al. (2020) note how certain aspects of motion capturing (MoCap) environments can lead to user discomfort and propose a lightweight marker setup, at the expense of a large number of cameras.

3. **(iii) Model development**

   As shown in Table 2, only one article described the involvement of deaf users in phase (iii). While practical challenges related to co-creation arise in this MT phase, the solution may lay within Principle 2 (the concept of a continuous, reflexive, and ongoing design process) and typological levels 4a, 4b, and 4c (such as the exchange of knowledge encompassing a wide range of expertise, and expanding the community as the project progresses), as well as Principle 9 (the complex dynamics of funding, formulating research goals, and community involvement) from Caselli et al. (2021). Through continuous dialogue about the needs of the SL user, the requirements of the model, and the technical possibilities, a consensus can be reached. This approach helps address the challenge of implementing co-creation in MT phase (iii), –the Model Development phase–, but also the communicative aspect in between SL user and/or the SLC, and academics. We ought to point out that the typical MT/ML model development requires the efforts of an expert – someone who is familiar with using computational tools and methods for the design, development and (hyperparameter) optimization of such models. The role of the *expert* and the *user* are distinct and it is therefore difficult to integrate the user in this phase. However, the work of (Fails and Olsen, 2003; Amershi et al., 2014) offers an alternative modeling strategy which involves the user more actively – interactive MLT development. Perhaps this phase should be decomposes into smaller, more regular training / validation cycles in which the users are involved.

4. **(iv) Quality assessment (automatic and / or human)**

   As shown in Table 2, we observe that in the current MT landscape, a significant amount of work (17 articles) involves users during evaluation, i.e. phase (iv). In these articles, the authors seek feedback primarily from deaf users (5 articles), linguists (2 articles), experts of unclear designation (2 articles), and a combination of Deaf and Hearing individuals (2 articles), as well as hearing, interpreters, interpreters and deaf and teachers (1 article each). These users have been asked to provide feedback on the outcomes and/ or results of the translation such as (Al-Khalifa, 2010; Chiu et al., 2007; Stein et al., 2006; Wu et al., 2007), with some being involved in multiple phases, particularly in phase (ii), in for example, (Khan et al., 2020; Luqman and Mahmoud, 2019; Müller et al., 2022; Rodríguez et al., 2020)). Thus, users appear to be involved in overlapping roles, such as data collection and/ or preparation, and MT system evaluation. While this is a solid starting point, we would like to highlight that continuous assessment across multiple MT phases can be beneficial for managing expectations and aligning participants and goals, i.e. following Principle 8 (The thin red line between consent and intrusion) and Principle 1 (Consensus and conflict) of (Caselli et al., 2021).

We ought to note that, as can be inferred from

Table 2, there exist collaboration and knowledge exchange between researchers, interpreters, experts (sometimes undefined), linguists, and teachers, while individuals who are Hard of Hearing (HoH) and Deaf have not been recognized and involved as language experts. However, historically and still to day, these collaborations are limited to certain distinct roles that do not align with Caselli et al. (2021)'s guidelines nor with Lepp et al. (2025)'s recommendations for effective co-creation. Recognizing that HoH and Deaf individuals are not only native[14] in their language, and therefore possess the most hands-on knowledge and experience, but are also the main end-users of SLMT systems who can steer the development of such technology, as well as expanding their involvement in future projects would allow for a more socially relevant translation technology.

4 Critical Reflection on User Involvement in SLMT Phases

The analysis of user involvement in the different phases of Sign Language Machine Translation (SLMT) reveals significant gaps in alignment with co-creation and participatory design best practices. While there has been progress in areas like data collection and evaluation, key phases such as problem definition and model development lack sufficient user input. This under representation not only affects the quality of the technology but raises ethical concerns about the exclusion of the very users SLMT is designed to serve.

Phase (i): Problem and Use-Case Definition User involvement in the early phase of problem definition and solution ideation is crucial to ensure that SLMT technologies address real-world needs. However, only one study (Morrissey and Way, 2007) reports any user involvement in this phase. This omission contradicts several co-creation principles (Caselli et al., 2021), such as the importance of early collaboration and continuous design iteration. Without user input at this stage, there is a risk that the technologies developed may not adequately reflect the needs and experiences of the Deaf and Hard of Hearing (HoH) communities, leading to solutions that are out of touch with real-world challenges.

Phase (ii): Dataset Construction SL users play a more substantial role in dataset construction, primarily through data collection, annotation, and recording. However, these tasks often place users in passive roles, with little involvement in designing the data collection process itself. This limits the potential for authentic and representative data. Research (e.g., (Vandeghinste et al., 2024)) shows that non-native signers or those unfamiliar with specific sign languages can distort data, leading to less accurate translations. A more participatory approach where users are actively involved in shaping data collection methods would help ensure the quality and authenticity of the datasets used for SLMT.

Phase (iii): Model Development Model development is a technically challenging phase, and only one study reports SL user involvement in this area. While experts are essential for model design and optimization, the limited involvement of SL users in this phase perpetuates a divide between technical expertise and user experience. Emerging approaches like interactive machine learning (Fails and Olsen, 2003; Amershi et al., 2014) suggest that more iterative, user-driven cycles of model development could better integrate user insights and improve the relevance of the technology.

Phase (iv): Quality Assessment In the quality assessment phase, SL users are most actively involved, with 17 studies seeking user feedback on translation outputs. However, this involvement is often limited to evaluation, without clear recognition of Deaf and HoH individuals as primary language experts. This oversight reduces the potential of user-driven insights. Additionally, feedback from users is often not integrated into earlier phases, preventing a continuous, cross-phase dialogue that could better align expectations and outcomes. A more integrated approach, where users contribute to evaluation across multiple phases, would ensure that SLMT systems better meet their needs.

5 Conclusion

Since its inception in the 1950s, a significant progress has been made in the field of Machine

[14]As Vandeghinste et al. (2024) indicate, the term "native" signer is an "ill-fitting label" and instead, the term "authentic" signers should be used. However, for parallels with "native" or L1 speakers, we chose to use this widely accepted formulation.

Translation (MT) for Spoken Languages reaching to human-like quality. However, the evolution of Sign Language Machine Translation (SLMT) has been slower due to a variety of challenges, including the complexity of data collection, modeling, as well as the intricate nature of human involvement. In contrast to SpL MT, where nowadays user involvement is often limited to data collection and evaluation, the inclusion of users of SLMT technology in all phases of SLMT research and development is quite important, although often overlooked. For example, in phase (i) users should be involved in order to identify the right use cases, and aid the ideation of a societal-relevant solution; in phase (ii) users should be involved to work on the data (record, annotate, guide); in phase (iv) users should be involved in evaluating the model and validating the solution. Phase (iii) requires expert knowledge to design, develop and validate a model; however, in line with the work on iterative ML (Fails and Olsen, 2003; Amershi et al., 2014), perhaps this phase should be broken down into smaller, more regular training/ validation cycles in which the users are involved. We leave testing this idea for future work.

To assess the current state of user involvement in SLMT, we analyzed 111 articles that were previously reviewed in (Núñez-Marcos et al., 2023; Coster et al., 2024). Our analysis reveals that user involvement in SLMT is still largely limited, with substantial participation in phases (ii) and (iv), that is – as content creators, monitors and evaluators but with minimal participation during early phases such as problem definition and model design. This lack of engagement can result in poorly aligned expectations, suboptimal outputs, and ethical concerns, particularly when non-signers are involved in data creation (as indicated, among others, by Buchan et al. (2017); Caselli et al. (2021); Morley et al. (2023)). To address these issues, we advocate for a more participatory approach, where SL users are integral collaborators, not just data providers or evaluators. This requires adjusting the roles of SL users to better reflect their expertise and ensuring that they are involved throughout the entire MT life cycle.

Overall, this work calls for a shift in how SLMT projects are approached, emphasizing the importance of co-creation and partnership with the SL user and SLCs to ensure that translation technologies are developed in a way that is both technically sound and socially responsible.

6 Author contributions

Conceptualization: L. Lepp;
Methodology: L. Lepp;
Validation: D. Shterionov;
Formal analysis: L. Lepp;
Investigation: L. Lepp;
Resources: L. Lepp, M. De Sisto, D. Shterionov;
Data curation: L. Lepp, M. De Sisto, D. Shterionov;
Writing – original draft: L. Lepp;
Writing – review and editing: L. Lepp, M. De Sisto, D. Shterionov;
Visualization: L. Lepp;
Supervision: M. De Sisto, D. Shterionov, G. Chrupała;
Project administration: M. De Sisto, D. Shterionov, G. Chrupała;
Funding acquisition: D. Shterionov and M. De Sisto.

References

Hend S. Al-Khalifa. 2010. Introducing arabic sign language for mobile phones. In *Computers Helping People with Special Needs*, pages 213–220, Berlin, Heidelberg. Springer.

Saleema Amershi, Maya Cakmak, W. Bradley Knox, and Todd Kulesza. 2014. Power to the people: The role of humans in interactive machine learning. *AI Mag.*, 35(4):105–120.

Dzmitry Bahdanau, Kyunghyun Cho, and Yoshua Bengio. 2015. Neural machine translation by jointly learning to align and translate. In *Proceedings of the 3rd International Conference on Learning Representations (ICLR 2015)*, San Diego, CA, USA. 15pp.

Jim Buchan, Muneera Bano, Didar Zowghi, Stephen MacDonell, and Amrita Shinde. 2017. Alignment of stakeholder expectations about user involvement in agile software development. In *Proceedings of the 21st International Conference on Evaluation and Assessment in Software Engineering*, EASE '17, page 334–343, New York, NY, USA. Association for Computing Machinery.

Tommaso Caselli, Roberto Cibin, Costanza Conforti, Enrique Encinas, and Maurizio Teli. 2021. Guiding principles for participatory design-inspired natural language processing. In *Proceedings of the 1st Workshop on NLP for Positive Impact*, pages 27–35, Online. Association for Computational Linguistics.

Yu-Hsien Chiu, Chung-Hsien Wu, Hung-Yu Su, and Chih-Jen Cheng. 2007. Joint optimization of word alignment and epenthesis generation for chinese to taiwanese sign synthesis. *IEEE Trans. Pattern Anal. Mach. Intell.*, 29(1):28–39.

Mathieu De Coster, Mieke Van Herreweghe, and Joni Dambre. 2019. Towards automatic sign language corpus annotation using deep learning. In *6th Workshop on Sign Language Translation and Avatar Technology (SLTAT)*, page 3.

Mathieu De Coster, Dimitar Shterionov, Mieke Van Herreweghe, and Joni Dambre. 2024. Machine translation from signed to spoken languages: state of the art and challenges. *Univers. Access Inf. Soc.*, 23(3):1305–1331.

Maartje De Meulder. 2021. Is "good enough" good enough? ethical and responsible development of sign language technologies. In *Proceedings of the 1st International Workshop on Automatic Translation for Signed and Spoken Languages (AT4SSL)*, pages 12–22, Virtual. Association for Machine Translation in the Americas.

Aashaka Desai, Maartje de Meulder, Julie A. Hochgesang, Annemarie Kocab, and Alex X. Lu. 2024. Systemic biases in sign language AI research: A deaf-led call to reevaluate research agendas. *CoRR*, abs/2403.02563.

Zijian Ding, Alison Smith-Renner, Wenjuan Zhang, Joel Tetreault, and Alejandro Jaimes. 2023. Harnessing the power of LLMs: Evaluating human-AI text co-creation through the lens of news headline generation. In *Findings of the Association for Computational Linguistics: EMNLP 2023*, pages 3321–3339, Singapore. Association for Computational Linguistics.

Sarah Ebling and Matt Huenerfauth. 2015. Bridging the gap between sign language machine translation and sign language animation using sequence classification. pages 2–9.

Jerry Alan Fails and Dan R. Olsen. 2003. Interactive machine learning. In *Proceedings of the 8th International Conference on Intelligent User Interfaces*, IUI '03, page 39–45, New York, NY, USA. Association for Computing Machinery.

Hugo Gonçalo Oliveira, Tiago Mendes, and Ana Boavida. 2017. Co-PoeTryMe: a co-creative interface for the composition of poetry. In *Proceedings of the 10th International Conference on Natural Language Generation*, pages 70–71, Santiago de Compostela, Spain. Association for Computational Linguistics.

Marie K. Harder, Gemma Burford, and Elona Hoover. 2013. What Is Participation? Design Leads the Way to a Cross-Disciplinary Framework. *Design Issues*, 29(4):41–57.

Pavel Jedlička, Zdeněk Krňoul, Jakub Kanis, and Miloš Železný. 2020. Sign language motion capture dataset for data-driven synthesis. In *Proceedings of the LREC2020 9th Workshop on the Representation and Processing of Sign Languages: Sign Language Resources in the Service of the Language Community, Technological Challenges and Application Perspectives*, pages 101–106, Marseille, France. European Language Resources Association (ELRA).

Nabeel Sabir Khan, Adnan Abid, and Kamran Abid. 2020. A novel natural language processing (nlp)–based machine translation model for english to pakistan sign language translation. *Cognitive Computation*, 12(4):748–765.

Kai Konen, Sophie Jentzsch, Diaoulé Diallo, Peer Schütt, Oliver Bensch, Roxanne El Baff, Dominik Opitz, and Tobias Hecking. 2024. Style vectors for steering generative large language models. In *Findings of the Association for Computational Linguistics: EACL 2024*, pages 782–802, St. Julian's, Malta. Association for Computational Linguistics.

Lisa Lepp, Dimitar Shterionov, Mirella De Sisto, and Grzegorz Chrupała. 2025. Co-Creation for Sign Language Processing and Translation Technology. *Information*, 16(4).

Verónica López-Ludeña, Rubén San Segundo, Juan Manuel Montero, Ricardo de Córdoba, Javier Ferreiros, and José Manuel Pardo. 2012. Automatic categorization for improving spanish into spanish sign language machine translation. *Comput. Speech Lang.*, 26(3):149–167.

Hamzah Luqman and Sabri A. Mahmoud. 2019. Automatic translation of Arabic text-to-Arabic sign language. *Universal Access in the Information Society*, 18(4):939–951.

Enrique Manjavacas, Folgert Karsdorp, Ben Burtenshaw, and Mike Kestemont. 2017. Synthetic literature: Writing science fiction in a co-creative process. In *Proceedings of the Workshop on Computational Creativity in Natural Language Generation (CC-NLG 2017)*, pages 29–37, Santiago de Compostela, Spain. Association for Computational Linguistics.

Ian Marshall and Éva Sáfár. 2002. Sign language generation using HPSG. In *Proceedings of the 9th Conference on Theoretical and Methodological Issues in Machine Translation of Natural Languages: Papers*, Keihanna, Japan.

Jessica Morley, Libby Kinsey, Anat Elhalal, Francesca Garcia, Marta Ziosi, and Luciano Floridi. 2023. Operationalising AI ethics: barriers, enablers and next steps. *AI Soc.*, 38(1):411–423.

Sara Morrissey and Andy Way. 2007. Joining hands: Developing A sign language machine translation system with and for the deaf community. In *Proceedings of the Conference and Workshop on Assistive Technologies for People with Vision and Hearing Impairments: Assistive Technology for All Ages (CVHI-2007), Granada, Spain, 28th - 31th August, 2007*, volume 415 of *CEUR Workshop Proceedings*. CEUR-WS.org.

Mathias Müller, Sarah Ebling, Eleftherios Avramidis, Alessia Battisti, Michèle Berger, Richard Bowden, Annelies Braffort, Necati Cihan Camgöz, Cristina España-Bonet, Roman Grundkiewicz, Zifan Jiang,

Oscar Koller, Amit Moryossef, Regula Perrollaz, Sabine Reinhard, Annette Rios, Dimitar Shterionov, Sandra Sidler-Miserez, and Katja Tissi. 2022. Findings of the first WMT shared task on sign language translation (WMT-SLT22). In *Proceedings of the Seventh Conference on Machine Translation, WMT 2022, Abu Dhabi, United Arab Emirates (Hybrid), December 7-8, 2022*, pages 744–772. Association for Computational Linguistics.

Takao Nakaguchi, Masayuki Otani, Toshiyuki Takasaki, and Toru Ishida. 2016. Combining human inputters and language services to provide multi-language support system for international symposiums. In *Proceedings of the Third International Workshop on Worldwide Language Service Infrastructure and Second Workshop on Open Infrastructures and Analysis Frameworks for Human Language Technologies (WLSI/OIAF4HLT2016)*, pages 28–35, Osaka, Japan. The COLING 2016 Organizing Committee.

Adrián Núñez-Marcos, Olatz Perez-de-Viñaspre, and Gorka Labaka. 2023. A survey on Sign Language Machine Translation. *Expert Syst. Appl.*, 213(Part):118993.

Franz Josef Och and Hermann Ney. 2003. A systematic comparison of various statistical alignment models. *Computational Linguistics*, 29(1):19–51.

Jefferson Rodríguez, Juan Chacón, Edgar Rangel, Luis Guayacán, Claudia Hernández, Luisa Hernández, and Fabio Martínez. 2020. Understanding motion in sign language: A new structured translation dataset. In *Computer Vision - ACCV 2020 - 15th Asian Conference on Computer Vision, Kyoto, Japan, November 30 - December 4, 2020, Revised Selected Papers, Part VI*, volume 12627 of *Lecture Notes in Computer Science*, pages 669–684. Springer.

Ashish Sharma, Sudha Rao, Chris Brockett, Akanksha Malhotra, Nebojsa Jojic, and Bill Dolan. 2024. Investigating agency of LLMs in human-AI collaboration tasks. In *Proceedings of the 18th Conference of the European Chapter of the Association for Computational Linguistics (Volume 1: Long Papers)*, pages 1968–1987, St. Julian's, Malta. Association for Computational Linguistics.

Dimitar Shterionov, Lorraine Leeson, and Andy Way. 2024. *The Pipeline of Sign Language Machine Translation*, pages 1–25. Springer Nature Switzerland, Cham.

Mirella De Sisto, Vincent Vandeghinste, Santiago Egea Gómez, Mathieu De Coster, Dimitar Shterionov, and Horacio Saggion. 2022. Challenges with sign language datasets for sign language recognition and translation. In *Proceedings of the Thirteenth Language Resources and Evaluation Conference, LREC 2022, Marseille, France, 20-25 June 2022*, pages 2478–2487. European Language Resources Association.

Daniel Stein, Jan Bungeroth, and Hermann Ney. 2006. Morpho-syntax based statistical methods for automatic sign language translation. In *European Association for Machine Translation Conferences/Workshops*.

Vincent Vandeghinste, Mirella De Sisto, Santiago Egea Gómez, and Mathieu De Coster. 2024. *Challenges with Sign Language Datasets*, pages 117–139. Springer Nature Switzerland, Cham.

Chung-Hsien Wu, Hung-Yu Su, Yu-Hsien Chiu, and Chia-Hung Lin. 2007. Transfer-based statistical translation of taiwanese sign language using PCFG. *ACM Trans. Asian Lang. Inf. Process.*, 6(1):1.

A Lepp et al.'s typology

The typology of Lepp et al. (2025) is shown in Table 3. [15]

B Caselli et al.'s principles

1. **PD is about consensus and conflict.** The design of co-creation should be conducted in discussion and alignment between the involved parties.

2. **Design is an inherently disordered and unfinished process.** The design should be a continuous, reflexive and ongoing process (principle 2 and 6 of (Caselli et al., 2021) and level 4c of our proposed typology in Table 3. (Caselli et al., 2021) mention that the term *community* needs to be defined in a reflexive and adaptable manner, with its continuous changes.(Harder et al., 2013) assume that this definition is a fixed format, based on the amount of *power* of different researchers (i.e. hearing, HoH or deaf) to define the SLC.

3. Communities are often **not determined** *a priori.*

4. **Data and communities are not separate things** Principle 4 of (Caselli et al., 2021) contain the assumption that we expect that communities have a prominent role in the development of NLP-systems, but that the communities until now most often only function as language data providers. This assumption raises the question where the separation line between SL-user and researchers is, or in which cases the SL-user indeed only provides data. In the last case we can categorize this on level 2 of (Harder et al., 2013).

5. **Community involvement is not scraping** In principle 5, the social interactions are described as necessary for the creation or development of a tool for a specific community, wherein also the ethical engagements, equity, reciprocity, and respect should be discussed. As Level 4.b. and level 4.c assume that working together in equality, with clear ethical practices are already described, this principle is also hard to divide to one level. Ideally suited -yes- working on equal level is the highest possible achievement, although in most of the current SLMT projects this step is not implemented or discussed. The development of the expectations/ ethical engagement should be on level 3 (as this part is meant as learning from each others needs) or level 4 (in discussion with each other), and if this is already discussed and decided, then this principle can be divided into level 4b or level 4c for the execution. But also in this case, a reciprocity attitude is needed for reflection and adaption of execution.

6. **Never stop designing** Principle 6 states out that when a NLP-tool is based on PD, there should be awareness about the needs of the SLC and include them into the design stage. By including them, technical and resource issues can be decreased, and participants effort can be recognized as labor.

7. **Language[16] is a means rather than an end.** Principle 7 refers to switch the perspective from *language as data* to *language as people*, wherein the main focus should be to serve people's needs instead of trying to copy people's language use. This principle can ideally be compared with level 4b (Growing as one) or level 4c (Working as one), but in most of the current SLMT this principle is comparable with level 2 -as the researchers need the SLC for this perspective-switch- or level 3, wherein both parties have a discussion and consensus about which perspective is followed.

8. **The thin red line between consent and intrusion** Principle 8 can be part of some of the lower levels already - as soon as some form of recognition of language as people is formed, so this principle can be seen as 'learning about' (level 1) or 'Learning from (Level 2).

9. **The need to combine research goals, funding and societal political dynamics.** The last principle - principle 9 - refers to the complex dynamics of funding (for projects that support co-creation with the community), goals of the research projects, and the community itself. As the most SLMT-projects are not supported

[15]The table is added in this article with the agreement of all authors of Lepp et al. (2025).

[16]Please be aware that in the article of (Caselli et al., 2021) the original principle is *Text is a means rather than an end*, that we have more specified in this article to language.

Level (-1)		Level (0)	Level (1)	Level (2)	Level (3)	Level (4)		
Denigration direct impact	*Denigration indirect impact*	*Neglect*	*Learning about*	*Learning from*	*Learning together*	*Learning as one*	*Growing as one*	*Working as one*
Hearing researchers make decisions without the SLC (neither HoH or deaf researchers) involvement, contrary to the SLCs interests, producing outputs with direct impact on the SLC.	Hearing researchers make decisions without the SLC (neither HoH or deaf researchers) involvement, contrary to or unaware of the SLCs interests, producing outputs with no direct impact on the SLC.	Hearing researchers make decisions without the SLC (neither HoH or Dear researchers) involvement, ignorant or dismissive of the SLCs interests.	Hearing researchers ask the SLCs and the users (and/or HoH or deaf researchers) opinions, but do not necessarily take them into account: the hearing researchers make the final decisions.	Hearing researchers ask the SLCs and the users opinions and consider the SLCs and users seriously. Hearing researchers still makes the final decision based on the information, HoH and deaf researchers are asked for evaluation, but not included in the process.	Major objectives and issues are discussed / negotiated jointly involving hearing, HoH and deaf researchers, and SL users. Most decisions are made jointly, e.g. by consensus-building.	A consortium that includes hearing, HoH and deaf researchers, and SLC members, jointly built, discuss relevant issues by having knowledge exchange (e.g. seminars on different topics from all involved communities).	Hearing, HoH and deaf researchers, and SL users work together on equal basis, are all integrated into the scope of the research cycle, but the SL user is not involved in the execution of each step and / or the societal diversity is not representative.	Hearing, HoH and deaf researchers, and SL users have a full consensus about the practices, the design is a continuous process and both the hearing researchers as well as the SL users are equally integrated into the scope, depth and breadth of the research project.

Table 3: Advanced typology of participation relationships of Lepp et al. (2025).

by a grand for the above needed adaptations, this principle can be compared to level 1 or level 2.

C Paper reviews

1. Angelova, G., Avramidis, E., Möller, S.: Using neural machine translation methods for sign language translation. In: Proceedings of the 60th Annual Meeting of the Association for Computational Linguistics: Student Research Workshop, pp. 273–284 (2022) Deaf involvement: no Evaluation: there are no deaf people involved: only focus on the MT-process. Level -1 Level: -1 b Depth: Only (hearing) researchers Breadth: No different groups/ variations are involved Scope: In none of the research life cycle steps

2. Arvanitis, N., Constantinopoulos, C., Kosmopoulos, D.: Translation of sign language glosses to text using sequence-to-sequence attention models. In: 2019 15th International Conference on Signal-Image Technology & Internet-Based Systems (SITIS), pp. 296–302 (2019). `https://doi.org/10.1109/SITIS.2019.00056`. IEEE Deaf involvement: no Evaluation: there are no deaf people involved: only focus on the MT-process. Level -1 Level: -1 b Depth: Only (hearing) researchers Breadth: No different groups/ variations are involved Scope: In none of the research life cycle steps

3. Barberis, D., Garazzino, N., Prinetto, P., Tiotto, G., Savino, A., Shoaib, U., et al. (2011). Language resources for computer assisted translation from italian to italian sign language of deaf people. In Proceedings of accessibility reaching everywhere AEGIS workshop and international conference (pp. 96–104). Deaf involvement: Yes, an interpret that helped in the production of signs Evaluation: there are no deaf people involved: only focus on the MT-process. Level -1 Level: -1 b Depth: Only (hearing) researchers Breadth: No different groups/ variations are involved Scope: In none of the research life cycle steps

4. Bauer, B., Nießen, S., & Hienz, H. (1999). Towards an automatic sign language translation system. In In 1st international. Citeseer. Deaf involvement: Yes, 1 DGS interpreter Evaluation: there are no deaf people involved, only one hearing interpreter for data recordings/ collection Level: -1 b Depth: Only (hearing) researchers Breadth: No different groups/ variations are involved Scope: In none of the research life cycle steps

5. Brour, M., & Benabbou, A. (2019). ATLASLang MTS 1: Arabic text language into Arabic Sign Language machine translation system. Procedia Computer Science, 148, 236–245. Deaf involvement: No Evaluation: there are no deaf people involved: only focus on the MT-process. Level -1 Level: -1 b Depth: Only (hearing) researchers Breadth: No different groups/ variations are involved Scope: In none of the research life cycle steps

6. Bungeroth, J., Ney, H.: Statistical sign language translation. In: Workshop on Representation and Processing of Sign Languages, LREC, vol. 4, pp. 105–108 (2004). Citese Deaf involvement: No Evaluation: there are no deaf people involved: only focus on the MT-process.

Level -1 Level: -1 b Depth: Only (hearing) researchers Breadth: No different groups/ variations are involved Scope: In none of the research life cycle steps

7. Camgoz, N. C., Koller, O., Hadfield, S., & Bowden, R. (2020a). Multi-channel trans- formers for multi-articulatory sign language translation. In European conference on computer vision (pp. 301–319). Springer. Deaf involvement: No Evaluation: there are no deaf people involved: only focus on the MT-process. Level -1 Level: -1 b Depth: Only (hearing) researchers Breadth: No different groups/ variations are involved Scope: In none of the research life cycle steps

8. Camgoz, N.C., Koller, O., Hadfield, S., Bowden, R.: Sign lan- guage transformers: Joint end-to-end sign language recognition and translation. In: Proceedings of the IEEE/CVF Conference on Computer Vision and Pattern Recognition, pp. 10023–10033 (2020) Deaf involvement: Yes, the existing 9 DGS-signers of the dataset Evaluation: there are no deaf people involved: only focus on the MT-process. Level -1 Level: -1 b Depth: Only (hearing) researchers Breadth: No different groups/ variations are involved Scope: In none of the research life cycle steps

9. Cao, Y., Li, W., Li, X., Chen, M., Chen, G., Hu, L., et al. (2022). Explore more guidance: A task-aware instruction network for sign language translation enhanced with data augmentation. arXiv preprint arXiv:2204.05953. Deaf involvement: no Evaluation: there are no deaf people involved: only focus on the MT-process. Level -1 Level: -1 b Depth: Only (hearing) researchers Breadth: No different groups/ variations are involved Scope: In none of the research life cycle steps

10. Chaudhary, L., Ananthanarayana, T., Hoq, E., Nwogu, I.: Signnet ii: A transformer-based two-way sign language translation model. IEEE Transactions on Pattern Analysis and Machine Intelligence (2022) Deaf involvement: no Evaluation: there are no deaf people involved: only focus on the MT-process. Level -1 Level: -1 b Depth: Only (hearing) researchers Breadth: No different groups/ variations are involved Scope: In none of the research life cycle steps

11. Chen, Y., Wei, F., Sun, X., Wu, Z., & Lin, S. (2022). A simple multi-modality transfer learning baseline for sign language translation. In Proceedings of the IEEE/CVF conference on computer vision and pattern recognition (pp. 5120–5130). Deaf involvement: no Evaluation: there are no deaf people involved: only focus on the MT-process. Level -1 Level: -1 b Depth: Only (hearing) researchers Breadth: No different groups/ variations are involved Scope: In none of the research life cycle steps

12. Chen, Y., Zuo, R., Wei, F., Wu, Y., Liu, S., Mak, B.: Two-stream network for sign language recognition and translation. arXiv pre- print arXiv: 2211. 01367 (2022) Deaf involvement: no Evaluation: there are no deaf people involved: only focus on the MT-process. Level -1 Level: -1 b Depth: Only (hearing) researchers Breadth: No different groups/ variations are involved Scope: In none of the research life cycle steps

13. De Meulder, Bert and Van Landuyt, Marleen and Omardeen, Sadiq: Systemic Biases in Sign Language AI Research: A Deaf-Led Call to Reevaluate Research Agendas. arXiv preprint arXiv:2408.13171 (2024)

14. D'Haro, L. F., San-Segundo, R., Cordoba, R. d., Bungeroth, J., Stein, D., & Ney, H. (2008). Language model adaptation for a speech to sign language translation system using web frequencies and a map framework. In Ninth annual conference of the international speech communication association. Deaf involvement: no Evaluation: there are no deaf people involved: only focus on the MT-process. Level -1 Level: -1 b Depth: Only (hearing) researchers Breadth: No different groups/ variations are involved Scope: In none of the research life cycle steps

15. Dasgupta, T., & Basu, A. (2008). Prototype machine translation system from text-to- Indian sign language. In Proceedings of the 13th international conference on intelligent user interfaces (pp. 313–316). Deaf involvement: No Evaluation: we have evaluated the sys?tem based on the feedbacks of the ISL experts Level: -1 b Depth: Only (hearing) researchers Breadth: No different groups/ variations are involved Scope: In none of the research life cycle steps

16. Davydov, M., & Lozynska, O. (2017a). Information system for translation into Ukrainian sign language on mobile devices. In 2017 12th international scientific and technical conference on computer sciences and information technologies, Vol. 1 CSIT, (pp. 48–51). IEEE. Deaf involvement: No Evaluation: there are no deaf people involved: only focus on the MT-process. Level -1 Level: -1 b Depth: Only (hearing) researchers Breadth: No different groups/ variations are involved Scope: In none of the research life cycle steps

17. De Coster, M., D'Oosterlinck, K., Pizurica, M., Rabaey, P., Ver- linden, S., Van Herreweghe, M., Dambre, J.: Frozen pretrained transformers for neural sign language translation. In: Proceedings of the 1st International Workshop on Automatic Translation for Signed and Spoken Languages (AT4SSL), pp. 88–97. Association for Machine Translation in the Americas, Virtual (2021). Deaf involvement: No Evaluation: there are no deaf people involved: only focus on the MT-process. Level -1, but the authors mention that 'co-creation with the DHH community members is the key'. Level: -1 b Depth: Only (hearing) researchers Breadth: No different groups/ variations are involved Scope: In none of the research life cycle steps

18. De Coster, M., Dambre, J.: Leveraging frozen pretrained written language models for neural sign language translation. Informa- tion 13(5), 220 (2022) Deaf involvement: no Evaluation: there are no deaf people involved: only focus on the MT-process. Level -1 Level: -1 b Depth: Only (hearing) researchers Breadth: No different groups/ variations are involved Scope: In none of the research life cycle steps

19. Dey, S., Pal, A., Chaabani, C., Koller, O.: Clean text and full- body transformer: Microsoft's submission to the wmt22 shared task on sign language translation. In: Proceedings of the Seventh Conference on Machine Translation, pp. 969–976. Association for Computational Linguistics, Abu Dhabi (2022). https://aclanthology.org/2022.wmt-1.93 Deaf involvement: No (at least not clear mentioned: the authors mention something about human evaluation, but it seems that that is out of the scope of this article). Evaluation: there are no deaf people involved: only focus on the MT-process. Level -1 Level: -1 b Depth: Only (hearing) researchers Breadth: No different groups/ variations are involved Scope: In none of the research life cycle steps

20. Dreuw, P., Stein, D., Deselaers, T., Rybach, D., Zahedi, M., Bungeroth, J., Ney, H.: Spoken language processing techniques for sign language recognition and translation. Technol. Disabil. 20(2), 121–133 (2008) Deaf involvement: no Evaluation: there are no deaf people involved: only focus on the MT-process. Level -1 Level: -1 b Depth: Only (hearing) researchers Breadth: No different groups/ variations are involved Scope: In none of the research life cycle steps

21. Dreuw, P., Stein, D., Deselaers, T., Rybach, D., Zahedi, M., Bungeroth, J., et al. (2008). Spoken language processing techniques for sign language recognition and translation. Technology and Disability, 20(2), 121–133. Deaf involvement: no Evaluation: there are no deaf people involved: only focus on the MT-process. Level -1 Level: -1 b Depth: Only (hearing) researchers Breadth: No different groups/ variations are involved Scope: In none of the research life cycle steps

22. Dreuw, P., Stein, D., Ney, H.: Enhancing a sign language transla- tion system with vision-based features. In: International Gesture Workshop, pp. 108–113 (2007). Springer Deaf involvement: no Evaluation: there are no deaf people involved: only focus on the MT-process. Level -1 Level: -1 b Depth: Only (hearing) researchers Breadth: No different groups/ variations are involved Scope: In none of the research life cycle steps

23. Egea, S., McGill, E., & Saggion, H. (2021). Syntax-aware transformers for neural machine translation: The case of text to sign gloss translation. In Proceedings of the 14th workshop on building and using comparable corpora. Deaf involvement: no Evaluation: there are no deaf people involved: only focus on the MT-process. Level -1 Level: -1 b Depth: Only (hearing) researchers Breadth: No different groups/ variations are involved Scope: In none of the research life cycle steps

24. Fang, B., Co, J., & Zhang, M. (2017). DeepASL: Enabling ubiquitous and non-intrusive word and sentence-level sign language translation. In Proceedings of the 15th ACM conference on embedded network sensor systems (pp. 1–13). Deaf involvement: 11 hearing participants who learned ASL via 3-hours tutorials Evaluation: level -1: contrary to the SLCs interests) 11 hearing participants who learnerd ASL via 3-hours tutorials Level: -1 a Depth: Only (hearing) researchers Breadth: No different groups/ variations are involved Scope: In none of the research life cycle steps

25. Foong, O. M., Low, T. J., & La, W. W. (2009). V2s: Voice to sign language translation system for malaysian deaf people. In International visual informatics conference (pp. 868–876). Springer. Deaf involvement: Yes, 100 people (groups of children, male, female, young and older), but no deaf. Evaluation: It is not focused on SL, but on SpLs Level: -1 b Depth: Only (hearing) researchers Breadth: No different groups / variations are involved Scope: In none of the research life cycle steps

26. Forster, J., Schmidt, C., Hoyoux, T., Koller, O., Zelle, U., Piater, J.H., Ney, H.: Rwth-phoenix-weather: A large vocabu?lary sign language recognition and translation corpus. In: LREC, vol. 9, pp. 3785–3789 (2012) Deaf involvement: It was not implemented Evaluation: there are no deaf people involved: only focus on the MT-process. Level -1 Level: -1 a Depth: Only (hearing) researchers Breadth: No different groups/ variations are involved Scope: In none of the research life cycle steps

27. Forster, J., Schmidt, C., Koller, O., Bellgardt, M., Ney, H.: Exten- sions of the sign language recognition and translation corpus rwth-phoenix-weather. In: LREC, pp. 1911–1916 (2014) Deaf involvement: no Evaluation: there are no deaf people involved: only focus on the MT-process. Level -1 Level: -1 b Depth: Only (hearing) researchers Breadth: No different groups/ variations are involved Scope: In none of the research life cycle steps

28. Fu, B., Ye, P., Zhang, L., Yu, P., Hu, C., Chen, Y., et al. (2022). ConSLT: A token- level contrastive framework for sign language translation. arXiv preprint arXiv: 2204.04916. Deaf involvement: no Evaluation: there are no deaf people involved: only focus on the MT-process. Level -1 Level: -1 b Depth: Only (hearing) researchers Breadth: No different groups/ variations are involved Scope: In none of the research life cycle steps

29. Gan, S., Yin, Y., Jiang, Z., Xie, L., Lu, S.: Skeleton-aware neu- ral sign language translation. In: Proceedings of the 29th ACM International Conference on Multimedia, pp. 4353–4361 (2021) Deaf involvement: no Evaluation: there are no deaf people involved: only focus on the MT-process. Level -1 Level: -1 b Depth: Only (hearing) researchers Breadth: No different groups/ variations are involved Scope: In none of the research life cycle steps

30. Grieve-Smith, A. B. (1999). English to American Sign Language machine translation of weather reports. In Proceedings of the second high desert student conference in linguistics (HDSL2), Albuquerque, NM (pp. 23–30). Deaf involvement: No, althouh the author mention in future work that the ouput needs to be cross-checked with a native signer Evaluation: there are no deaf people involved: only focus on the MT-process. Level -1 Level: -1 b Depth: Only (hearing) researchers Breadth: No different groups/ variations are involved Scope: In none of the research life cycle steps

31. Grif, M. G., Korolkova, O. O., Demyanenko, Y. A., & Tsoy, Y. B. (2011). Development of computer sign language translation technology for deaf people. In Proceedings of 2011 6th international forum on strategic technology, Vol. 2 (pp. 674–677). IEEE. Deaf involvement: not clear Evaluation: there are no deaf people involved: only focus on the MT-process. Level -1 Level: -1 b Depth: Only (hearing) researchers Breadth: No different groups/ variations are involved Scope: In none of the research life cycle steps

32. Guo, D., Zhou, W., Li, A., Li, H., & Wang, M. (2019). Hierarchical recurrent deep fusion using adaptive clip summarization for sign language translation. IEEE Transactions on Image Processing, 29, 1575–1590. Deaf involvement: Evaluation: there are no deaf people involved: only focus on the MT-process. Level -1 Level: -1 b Depth: Only (hearing) researchers Breadth: No different groups/ variations are involved Scope: In none of the research life cycle steps

33. Halawani, S. M. (2008). Arabic sign language translation system on mobile de- vices. IJCSNS International Journal of Computer Science and Network Security, 8(1), 251–256. Deaf involvement: No Evaluation: there are no deaf people involved: only focus on the MT-process. Level -1 Level: -1 b Depth: Only (hearing) researchers Breadth: No different groups/ variations are involved Scope: In none of the research life cycle steps

34. Hoque, M. T., Rifat-Ut-Tauwab, M., Kabir, M. F., Sarker, F., Huda, M. N., & Abdullah-Al- Mamun, K. (2016). Automated bangla sign language translation system: Prospects, limitations and applications. In 2016 5th international conference on informatics, electronics and vision ICIEV, (pp. 856–862). IEEE. Deaf involvement: no Evaluation: there are no deaf people involved: only focus on the MT-process. Level -1 Level: -1 a Depth: Only (hearing) researchers Breadth: No different groups/ variations are involved Scope: In none of the research life cycle steps

35. Huang, J., Zhou, W., Zhang, Q., Li, H., Li, W.: Video-based sign language recognition without temporal segmentation. In: Proceedings of the AAAI Conference on Artifcial Intelligence, vol. 32 (2018) Deaf involvement: no Evaluation: there are no deaf people involved: only focus on the MT-process. Level -1 Level: -1 b Depth: Only (hearing) researchers Breadth: No different groups/ variations are involved Scope: In none of the research life cycle steps

36. Huenerfauth, M. (2004). A multi-path architecture for machine translation of english text into American Sign language animation. In Proceedings of the student research workshop at HLT-NAACL 2004 (pp. 25–30). Deaf involvement: no Evaluation: there are no deaf people involved: only focus on the MT-process. Level -1 Level: -1 b Depth: Only (hearing) researchers Breadth: No different groups/ variations are involved Scope: In none of the research life cycle steps

37. Jin, T., Zhao, Z., Zhang, M., Zeng, X.: Mc-slt: Towards low- resource signer-adaptive sign language translation. In: Proceed- ings of the 30th ACM International Conference on Multimedia, pp. 4939–4947 (2022) Deaf involvement: no Evaluation: there are no deaf people involved: only focus on the MT-process. Level -1 Level: -1 b Depth: Only (hearing) researchers Breadth: No different groups/ variations are involved Scope: In none of the research life cycle steps

38. Jin, T., Zhao, Z., Zhang, M., Zeng, X.: Prior knowledge and memory enriched transformer for sign language translation. In: Findings of the Association for Computational Linguistics: ACL 2022, pp. 3766–3775 (2022) Deaf involvement: no Evaluation: there are no deaf people involved: only focus on the MT-process. Level -1 Level: -1 b Depth: Only (hearing) researchers Breadth: No different groups/ variations are involved Scope: In none of the research life cycle steps

39. Kamata, K., Yoshida, T., Watanabe, M., & Usui, Y. (1989). An approach to Japanese-sign language translation system. In Conference proceedings., IEEE international conference on systems, man and cybernetics (pp. 1089–1090). IEEE Deaf involvement: no Evaluation: there are no deaf people involved: only focus on the MT-process. Level -1 Level: -1 b Depth: Only (hearing) researchers Breadth: No different groups/ variations are involved Scope: In none of the research life cycle steps

40. Kan, J., Hu, K., Hagenbuchner, M., Tsoi, A.C., Bennamoun, M., Wang, Z.: Sign language translation with hierarchical spatio- temporal graph neural network. In: Proceedings of the IEEE/ CVF Winter Conference on Applications of Computer Vision, pp. 3367–3376 (2022) Deaf involvement: no Evaluation: there are no deaf people involved: only focus on the MT-process. Level -1 Level: -1 b Depth: Only (hearing) researchers Breadth: No different groups/ variations are involved Scope: In none of the research life cycle steps

41. Kim, S., Kim, C.J., Park, H.-M., Jeong, Y., Jang, J.Y., Jung, H.: Robust keypoint normalization method for korean sign language translation using transformer. In: 2020 International Conference on Information and Communication Technology Convergence (ICTC), pp. 1303–1305 (2020). https://doi.org/10.1109/ICTC49870.2020.9289551. IEEE Deaf involvement: Yes, for training (16 signers) and testing of data (4) Evaluation: there are no deaf people involved: only focus on the MT-process. Level -1 Level: -1 b Depth: Only (hearing) researchers Breadth: No different groups/ variations are involved Scope: In none of the research life cycle steps

42. Kouremenos, D., Ntalianis, K., & Kollias, S. 2018. A novel rule based machine translation scheme from Greek to Greek sign language: Production of different types of large corpora and language models evaluation. 51, 110–135, Deaf involvement: No Evaluation: level -1. A translator, Human evaluation is fundamental and remains of crucial importance to proper assessment of the quality of MT systems. When the output of an MT system is evaluated, however, the whole process is taken into account. In our case, different aspects of the proposed RBMT system are evaluated such as: (a) all stages of development of the transfer rules, (b) accuracy of translation and (c) complexity.Thus, it cannot be understood by deaf people, who cannot read the Greek language. A complete MT system for the GSL should produce animations, while a genuine and proper evaluation should involve deaf people, measuring comprehension regarding the animated output Level: -1 b Depth: Only (hearing) researchers Breadth: No different groups/ variations are involved Scope: In none of the research life cycle steps

43. Kumar, S.S., Wangyal, T., Saboo, V., Srinath, R.: Time series neural networks for real time sign language translation. In: 2018 17th IEEE International Conference on Machine Learning and Applications (ICMLA), pp. 243–248 (2018). https://doi.org/10.1109/ICMLA.2018.00043. IEEE Deaf involvement: no Evaluation: there are no deaf people involved: only focus on the MT-process. Level -1 Level: -1 b Depth: Only (hearing) researchers Breadth: No different groups/ variations are involved Scope: In none of the research life cycle steps

44. Li, D., Xu, C., Yu, X., Zhang, K., Swift, B., Suominen, H., Li, H.: Tspnet: Hierarchical feature learning via temporal semantic pyramid for sign language translation. Adv. Neural. Inf. Process. Syst. 33, 12034–12045 (2020) Deaf involvement: no Evaluation: there are no deaf people involved: only focus on the MT-process. Level -1 Level: -1 b Depth: Only (hearing) researchers Breadth: No different groups/ variations are involved Scope: In none of the research life cycle steps

45. Li, R., Meng, L.: Sign language recognition and translation network based on multi-view data. Appl. Intell. 52(13), 14624– 14638 (2022) Deaf involvement: no Evaluation: there are no deaf people involved: only focus on the MT-process. Level -1 Level: -1 b Depth: Only (hearing) researchers Breadth: No different groups/ variations are involved Scope: In none of the research life cycle steps

46. López-Ludeña, V., San-Segundo, R., Morcillo, C. G., López, J. C., & Muñoz, J. M. P. (2013). Increasing

adaptability of a speech into sign language translation system. Expert Systems with Applications, 40(4), 1312–1322. Deaf involvement: No Evaluation: there are no deaf people involved: only focus on the MT-process. Level -1 Level: -1 b Depth: Only (hearing) researchers Breadth: No different groups/ variations are involved Scope: In none of the research life cycle steps

47. Luqman, H., Mahmoud, S.A.: A machine translation system from arabic sign language to arabic. Univ. Access Inf. Soc. 19(4), 891–904 (2020). https://doi.org/10.1007/s10209-019-00695-6 Deaf involvement: no Evaluation: There are no deaf people involved: level -1. Evaluation by hearing Arab speakers for translation-evaluation (as the output is Arabic) Level: -1 b Depth: Only (hearing) researchers Breadth: No different groups/ variations are involved Scope: In none of the research life cycle steps

48. Marshall, I., & Sáfár, É. (2002). Sign language generation using HPSG. In Proceedings of the 9th Conference on Theoretical and Methodological Issues in Machine Translation of Natural Languages: Papers. Deaf involvement: No Evaluation: There are no deaf people involved (level -1) but the authors are aware of cco-creation: Sign research has frequently been carried out by hearing people using deaf informants and hence insights are typically second-hand. Additionally, the status of deaf informants themselves within the deaf community raises a significant issue. Typically only 5-10% of deaf people are born to deaf parents and thus are viewed as the genuine native signers who should act as informants and who should be asked to identify the preferred manner of signing a proposition rather than merely acceptable signing(Neidle et al. 2000). Deaf informants with hearing researchers and initial review by hearing signers are used to establish initial hypotheses. More extensive review by deaf users of the generated signing provides detailed feedback and guides revision. Level: -1 b Depth: Only (hearing) researchers Breadth: No different groups/ variations are involved Scope: In none of the research life cycle steps

49. Marshall, I., & Sáfár, É. (2003). A prototype text to British Sign Language (BSL) translation system. In The companion volume to the proceedings of 41st annual meeting of the association for computational linguistics (pp. 113–116). Deaf involvement: Evaluation: there are no deaf people involved: only focus on the MT-process. Level -1 Level: -1 b Depth: Only (hearing) researchers Breadth: No different groups/ variations are involved Scope: In none of the research life cycle steps

50. Miranda, P.B., Casadei, V., Silva, E., Silva, J., Alves, M., Severo, M., Freitas, J.P.: Tspnet-hf: A hand/face tspnet method for sign language translation. In: Ibero-American Conference on Artificial Intelligence, pp. 305–316 (2022). Springer Deaf involvement: no Evaluation: there are no deaf people involved: only focus on the MT-process. Level -1 Level: -1 b Depth: Only (hearing) researchers Breadth: No different groups/ variations are involved Scope: In none of the research life cycle steps

51. Mohamed, A., Hefny, H., et al.: A deep learning approach for gloss sign language translation using transformer. Journal of Computing and Communication 1(2), 1–8 (2022) Deaf involvement: no Evaluation: there are no deaf people involved: only focus on the MT-process. Level -1 Level: -1 b Depth: Only (hearing) researchers Breadth: No different groups/ variations are involved Scope: In none of the research life cycle steps

52. Morrissey, S. (2008). Assistive translation technology for deaf people: translating into and animating Irish sign language. Deaf involvement: Evaluation: there are no deaf people involved: only focus on the MT-process. Level -1 Level: -1 b Depth: Only (hearing) researchers Breadth: Only (hearing) researchers Scope: Only (hearing) researchers

53. Morrissey, S., & Way, A. (2005). An example-based approach to translating sign language. Deaf involvement: Evaluation: there are no deaf people involved: only focus on the MT-process. Level -1 Level: -1 b Depth: Only (hearing) researchers Breadth: No different groups/ variations are involved Scope: In none of the research life cycle steps

54. Morrissey, S., & Way, A. (2006). Lost in translation: the problems of using mainstream MT evaluation metrics for sign language translation Deaf involvement: The authors mention: Clearly, in addition, human evaluation remains crucial for all such approaches. Evaluation: there are no deaf people involved: only focus on the MT-process. Level -1 Level: -1 b Depth: Only (hearing) researchers Breadth: No different groups/ variations are involved Scope: In none of the research life cycle steps

55. Morrissey, S., Way, A., Stein, D., Bungeroth, J., Ney, H.: Com- bining data-driven mt systems for improved sign language trans- lation. In: European Association for Machine Translation (2007) Deaf involvement: no Evaluation: there are no deaf people involved: only focus on the MT-process. Level -1 Level: -1 b Depth: Only (hearing) researchers Breadth: No different groups/ variations are involved Scope: In none of the research life cycle steps

56. Moryossef, A., Yin, K., Neubig, G., Goldberg, Y.: Data aug- mentation for sign language gloss translation. In: Proceedings of the 1st International Workshop on Automatic Translation for Signed and Spoken Languages (AT4SSL), pp. 1–11. Association for Machine Translation in the Americas, Virtual (2021). https://aclanthology.org/2021.mtsummit-at4ssl.1 Deaf involvement: No Evaluation: there are no deaf people involved: only focus on the MT-process. Level -1 Level: -1 b Depth: Only (hearing) researchers Breadth: No different groups/ variations are involved Scope: In none of the research life cycle steps

57. Nießen, S., & Ney, H. (2004). Statistical machine translation with scarce resources using morpho-syntactic information. Computational Linguistics, 30(2), 181–204. Deaf involvement: no Evaluation: there are no deaf people involved: only focus on the MT-process. Level -1 Level: -1 b Depth: Only (hearing) researchers Breadth: No different groups/ variations are involved Scope: In none of the research life cycle steps

58. Orbay, A., Akarun, L.: Neural sign language translation by learn- ing tokenization. In: 2020 15th IEEE International Conference on Automatic Face and Gesture Recognition (FG 2020), pp. 222–228 (2020). IEEE Deaf involvement: No Evaluation: there are no deaf people involved: only focus on the MT-process. Level -1 Level: -1 b Depth: Only (hearing) researchers Breadth: No different groups/ variations are involved Scope: In none of the research life cycle steps

59. Othman, A., Jemni, M.: English-asl gloss parallel corpus 2012: Aslg-pc12. In: 5th Workshop on the Representation and Pro?cessing of Sign Languages: Interactions Between Corpus and Lexicon LREC (2012) Deaf involvement: No Evaluation: there are no deaf people involved: only focus on the MT-process. Level -1 Level: -1 b Depth: Only (hearing) researchers Breadth: No different groups/ variations are involved Scope: In none of the research life cycle steps

60. Partaourides, H., Voskou, A., Kosmopoulos, D., Chatzis, S., Metaxas, D.N.: Variational bayesian sequence-to-sequence net- works for memory-efficient sign language translation. In: Inter- national Symposium on Visual Computing, pp. 251–262 (2020). Springer Deaf involvement: no Evaluation: there are no deaf people involved: only focus on the MT-process. Level -1 Level: -1 b Depth: Only (hearing) researchers Breadth: No different groups/ variations are involved Scope: In none of the research life cycle steps

61. Porta, J., López-Colino, F., Tejedor, J., & Colás, J. (2014). A rule-based translation from written Spanish to Spanish Sign Language glosses. Computer Speech and Language, 28(3), 788–811. Deaf involvement: no Evaluation: Level -1 A parallel Spanish-LSE corpus has bvbeen created by two hearing interpreters (one of them was CODA) Level: -1 b Depth: Only (hearing) researchers Breadth: No different groups/ variations are involved Scope: In none of the research life cycle steps

62. Sáfár, É., & Marshall, I. (2001). The architecture of an english-text-to-sign-languages translation system. In Recent advances in natural language processing RANLP, (pp. 223–228). Tzigov Chark Bulgaria. Deaf involvement: Evaluation: there are no deaf people involved: only focus on the MT-process. Level -1 Level: -1 b Depth: Only (hearing) researchers Breadth: No different groups/ variations are involved Scope: In none of the research life cycle steps

63. Sáfár, É., & Marshall, I. (2002). Sign Language Translation via DRT and HPSG. Conference on Intelligent Text Processing and Computational Linguistics. Deaf involvement: No Evaluation: there are no deaf people involved: only focus on the MT-process. Level -1 Level: -1 b Depth: Only (hearing) researchers Breadth: No different groups/ variations are involved Scope: In none of the research life cycle steps

64. San Segundo, R., Pérez, A., Ortiz, D., Luis Fernando, D., Torres, M. I., & Casacuberta, F. (2007). Evaluation of alternatives on speech to sign language translation. In INTERSPEECH (pp. 2529–2532). Citeseer. Deaf involvement: No Evaluation: there are no deaf people involved: only focus on the MT-process. Level -1 Level: -1 b Depth: Only (hearing) researchers Breadth: No different groups/ variations are involved Scope: In none of the research life cycle steps

65. San-Segundo, R., Barra, R., Córdoba, R., D'Haro, L. F., Fernández, F., Ferreiros, J., et al. (2008). Speech to sign language translation system for Spanish. Speech Communication, 50(11–12), 1009–1020. Deaf involvement: No Evaluation: there are no deaf people involved: only focus on the MT-process. Level -1 Level: -1 b Depth: Only (hearing) researchers Breadth: No different groups/ variations are involved Scope: In none of the research life cycle steps

66. San-Segundo, R., Barra, R., D'Haro, L., Montero, J. M., Córdoba, R., & Ferreiros, J. (2006). A spanish speech to sign language translation system for assisting deaf-mute people. In Ninth international conference on spoken language processing. Deaf involvement: No Evaluation: there are no deaf people involved: only focus on the MT-process. Level -1 Level: -1 b Depth: Only (hearing) researchers Breadth: No different groups/ variations are involved Scope: In none of the research life cycle steps

67. Saunders, B., Camgoz, N. C., & Bowden, R. (2020b). Progressive transformers for end- to-end sign language production. In European conference on computer vision (pp. 687–705). Springer. Deaf involvement: No Evaluation: there are no deaf people involved: only focus on the MT-process. Level -1 Level: -1 b Depth: Only (hearing) researchers Breadth: No different groups/ variations are involved Scope: In none of the research life cycle steps

68. Schmidt, C., Koller, O., Ney, H., Hoyoux, T., Piater, J.: Using viseme recognition to improve a sign language translation sys?tem. In: International Workshop on Spoken Language Transla?tion, pp. 197–203 (2013). Citeseer Deaf involvement: No Evaluation: there are no deaf people involved: only focus on the MT-process. Level -1 Level: -1 b Depth: Only (hearing) researchers Breadth: No different groups/ variations are involved Scope: In none of the research life cycle steps

69. Stein, D., Dreuw, P., Ney, H., Morrissey, S., Way, A.: Hand in hand: automatic sign language to English translation. In: Proceedings of the 11th Conference on Theoretical and Methodological Issues in Machine Translation of Natural Languages: Papers, Skövde, Sweden (2007). https://aclanthology.org/2007.tmi-papers.26 Deaf involvement: No Evaluation: there are no deaf people involved: only focus on the MT-process. Level -1 Level: -1 b Depth: Only (hearing) researchers Breadth: No different groups/ variations are involved Scope: In none of the research life cycle steps

70. Stein, D., Schmidt, C., Ney, H.: Analysis, preparation, and opti?mization of statistical sign language machine translation. Mach. Transl. 26(4), 325–357 (2012) Deaf involvement: Evaluation: there are no deaf people involved: only focus on the MT-process. Level -1 Level: -1 b Depth: Only (hearing) researchers Breadth: No different groups/ variations are involved Scope: In none of the research life cycle steps

71. Stein, D., Schmidt, C., Ney, H.: Sign language machine transla- tion overkill. In: International Workshop on Spoken Language Translation (IWSLT) 2010 (2010) Deaf involvement: no Evaluation: there are no deaf people involved: only focus on the MT-process. Level - 1 Level: -1 b Depth: Only (hearing) researchers Breadth: No different groups/ variations are involved Scope: In none of the research life cycle steps

72. Stoll, S., Camgöz, N. C., Hadfield, S., & Bowden, R. (2018). Sign language production us- ing neural machine translation and generative adversarial networks. In Proceedings of the 29th British machine vision conference (BMVC 2018). University of Surrey. Deaf involvement: no Evaluation: there are no deaf people involved: only focus on the MT-process. Level -1 Level: -1 b Depth: Only (hearing) researchers Breadth: No different groups/ variations are involved Scope: In none of the research life cycle steps

73. Tarres, L., Gállego, G.I., Giro-i-Nieto, X., Torres, J.: Tackling low-resourced sign language translation: Upc at wmt-slt 22. In: Proceedings of the Seventh Conference on Machine Transla- tion, pp. 994–1000. Association for Computational Linguistics, Abu Dhabi (2022). https://aclanthology.org/2022.wmt-1.97 Deaf involvement: no Evaluation: there are no deaf people involved: only focus on the MT-process. Level -1 Level: -1 b Depth: Only (hearing) researchers Breadth: No different groups/ variations are involved Scope: In none of the research life cycle steps

74. Tokuda, M., & Okumura, M. (1998). Towards automatic translation from japanese into japanese sign language. In Assistive technology and artificial intelligence (pp. 97–108). Springer. Deaf involvement: No Evaluation: there are no deaf people involved: only focus on the MT-process. Level -1 Level: -1 b Depth: Only (hearing) researchers Breadth: No different groups/ variations are involved Scope: In none of the research life cycle steps

75. Wazalwar, S. S., & Shrawankar, U. (2017). Interpretation of sign language into English using NLP techniques. Journal of Information and Optimization Sciences, 38(6), 895–910. Deaf involvement: no Evaluation: The videos were interpretered by hearing teachers of school for the deaf Level -1 Level: -1 a Depth: Only (hearing) researchers Breadth: No different groups/ variations are involved Scope: In none of the research life cycle steps

76. Yin, A., Zhao, Z., Jin, W., Zhang, M., Zeng, X., He, X.: Mlslt: Towards multilingual sign language translation. In: Proceed- ings of the IEEE/CVF Conference on Computer Vision and Pattern Recognition, pp. 5109–5119 (2022) Deaf involvement: no Evaluation: there are no deaf people involved: only focus on the MT-process. Level -1 Level: -1 b Depth: Only (hearing) researchers Breadth: No different groups/ variations are involved Scope: In none of the research life cycle steps

77. Yin, A., Zhao, Z., Liu, J., Jin, W., Zhang, M., Zeng, X., He, X.: Simulslt: End-to-end simultaneous sign language translation. In: Proceedings of the 29th ACM International Conference on Mul- timedia, pp. 4118–4127 (2021) Deaf involvement: no Evaluation: there are no deaf people involved: only focus on the MT-process. Level -1 Level: -1 b Depth: Only (hearing) researchers Breadth: No different groups/ variations are involved Scope: In none of the research life cycle steps

78. Yin, K., Read, J.: Better sign language translation with stmc- transformer. In: Proceedings of the 28th International Conference on Computational Linguistics, pp. 5975–5989 (2020). https://doi.org/10.18653/v1/2020.coling-main.525 Deaf involvement: no Evaluation: there are no deaf people involved: only focus on the MT-process. Level -1 Level: -1 b Depth: Only (hearing) researchers Breadth: No different groups/ variations are involved Scope: In none of the research life cycle steps

79. Zhang, X., Duh, K.: Approaching sign language gloss translation as a low-resource machine translation task. In: Proceedings of the 1st International Workshop on Automatic Translation for Signed and Spoken Languages (AT4SSL), pp. 60–70. Association for Machine Translation in the Americas, Virtual (2021). https://aclanthology.org/2021.mtsummit-at4ssl.7 Deaf involvement: no Evaluation: there are no deaf people involved: only focus on the MT-process. Level -1 Level: -1 b Depth: Only (hearing) researchers Breadth: No different groups/ variations are involved Scope: In none of the research life cycle steps

80. Zhao, J., Qi, W., Zhou, W., Duan, N., Zhou, M., & Li, H. (2021). Conditional sentence generation and cross-modal reranking for sign language translation. IEEE Transactions on Multimedia, 24, 2662–2672. Deaf involvement: no Evaluation: there are no deaf people involved: only focus on the MT-process. Level -1 Level: -1 b Depth: Only (hearing) researchers Breadth: No different groups/ variations are involved Scope: In none of the research life cycle steps

81. Zhao, L., Kipper, K., Schuler, W., Vogler, C., Badler, N., & Palmer, M. (2000). A machine translation system from English to American sign language. In Conference of the association for machine translation in the Americas (pp. 54–67). Springer. Deaf involvement: no Evaluation: there are no deaf people involved: only focus on the MT-process. Level -1 Level: -1 b Depth: Only (hearing) researchers Breadth: No different groups/ variations are involved Scope: In none of the research life cycle steps

82. Zheng, J., Chen, Y., Wu, C., Shi, X., & Kamal, S. M. (2021). Enhancing neural sign lan- guage translation by highlighting the facial expression information. Neurocomputing, 464, 462–472. Deaf involvement: No Evaluation: there are no deaf people involved: only focus on the MT-process. Level -1 Level: -1 b Depth: Only (hearing) researchers Breadth: No different groups/ variations are involved Scope: In none of the research life cycle steps

83. Zheng, J., Zhao, Z., Chen, M., Chen, J., Wu, C., Chen, Y., Shi, X., Tong, Y.: An improved sign language translation model with explainable adaptations for processing long sign sentences. Com- putational Intelligence and Neuroscience 2020 (2020) Deaf involvement: no Evaluation: there are no deaf people involved: only focus on the MT-process. Level -1 Level: -1 b Depth: Only (hearing) researchers Breadth: No different groups/ variations are involved Scope: In none of the research life cycle steps

84. Zhou, H., Zhou, W., Zhou, Y., Li, H.: Spatial-temporal multi- cue network for sign language recognition and translation. IEEE Trans. Multimedia (2021). https://doi.org/10.1109/TMM.2021.3059098 Deaf involvement: no Evaluation: there are no deaf people involved: only focus on the MT-process. Level -1 Level: -1 b Depth: Only (hearing) researchers Breadth: No different groups/ variations are involved Scope: In none of the research life cycle steps

85. Baldassarri, S., Cerezo, E., & Royo-Santas, F. (2009). Automatic translation sys- tem to spanish sign language with a virtual interpreter. In IFIP conference on human-computer interaction (pp. 196–199). Springer. Deaf involvement: Yes, two teachers of a school for interpreters Evaluation: Level 0? Or level 1? Assessment was done by two teachers of a school of interpreters considering the accuracy of two aspects: the translation and the synthesis of the signs by the virtual interpreter. Level: 0 Depth: (hearing) researchers, SL-interpreters, but not the SL-user Breadth: little variation (not the SL-user involved) Scope: In the evaluation/ reflection phrase

86. Camgoz, N.C., Hadfield, S., Koller, O., Ney, H., Bowden, R.: Neural sign language translation. In: Proceedings of the IEEE Conference on Computer Vision and Pattern Recognition, pp. 7784–7793 (2018). https://doi.org/10.1109/CVPR.2018.00812 Deaf involvement: no Evaluation: Level 0. For the corpus, they used 9 different signers. Furthermore, the corpus annotations are made by SL-interpreters and deaf specialists. Level: 0 Depth: Breadth: Scope:

87. Camgöz, N.C., Saunders, B., Rochette, G., Giovanelli, M., Inches, G., Nachtrab-Ribback, R., Bowden, R.: Content4all open research sign language translation datasets. In: 2021 16th IEEE International Conference on Automatic Face and Gesture Recog- nition (FG 2021), pp. 1–5 (2021). https://doi.org/10.1109/FG52635.2021.9667087 Deaf involvement: Evaluation: Level 0. There were deaf experts and SL interpreters for the match ing of the SpLs text with the corresponding SL-video pairs, and annotation process Level: 0 Depth: Breadth: Scope:

88. Dal Bianco, P., Ríos, G., Ronchetti, F., Quiroga, F., Stanchi, O., Hasperué, W., Rosete, A.: Lsa-t: The first continuous argentinian sign language dataset for sign language translation. In: Ibero- American Conference on Artificial Intelligence, pp. 293–304 (2022). Springer Deaf involvement: no, a generated corpus from videos of YouTube Evaluation: Level 0. Videos of channel CN Sordos, a news channel created by deaf people and deaf people's relatives. 103 deaf signers as guests Level: 0 Depth: Breadth: Scope:

89. Ebling, S., & Huenerfauth, M. (2015). Bridging the gap between sign language machine translation and sign language animation using sequence classification. In Proceedings of SLPAT 2015: 6th workshop on speech and language processing for assistive technologies (pp. 2–9). Deaf involvement: Yes, deaf and hearing team members (translating) Evaluation: Yes, deaf and hearing team members (translating), but not clear to what exten (level 0) Level: 0 Depth: Breadth: Scope:

90. Ko, S.-K., Kim, C.J., Jung, H., Cho, C.: Neural sign language translation based on human keypoint estimation. Appl. Sci. 9(13), 2683 (2019) Deaf involvement: no Evaluation: level 0. 14 hearing-impaired for recordings (a copy of an 'expert' signing the requested signs, which the signers needed to copy) Level: 0 Depth: Breadth: Scope:

91. Krňoul, Z., Kanis, J., Železny, M., & Müller, L. (2007). Czech text-to-sign speech ' synthesizer. In International workshop on machine learning for multimodal interaction (pp. 180–191). Springer. Deaf involvement: two participants for the evaluation of the Sign Speech synthesizer Evaluation: Level 0. two experts in SignSpeech for the evaluation of the Sign Speech synthesizer Level: 0 Depth: Breadth: Scope:

92. Massó, G., & Badia, T. (2010). Dealing with sign language morphemes in statistical machine translation. In 4th workshop on the representation and processing of sign languages: Corpora and sign language technologies, Valletta, Malta (pp. 154–157). Matthes, S., Hanke, T., Regen, A., Storz, J., Worseck, S., Efthimiou, E., et al. (2012). Deaf involvement: No, the authors mention: Unfortunately, it was not possible to conduct a human evaluation by native deaf signers Evaluation: (level 0) The authors created a corpus based on Catalan Weather texts which were translated by a native deaf signer Level: 0 Depth: Breadth: Scope:

93. Moe, S.Z., Thu, Y.K., Thant, H.A., Min, N.W., Supnithi, T.: Unsupervised Neural Machine Translation between Myanmar Sign Language and Myanmar Language . TIC 14(15), 16 (2020) Deaf involvement: Yes, for data collection Evaluation: Level 0. 30 SL trainers and deaf people from different MSL dialects for data collection Level: 0 Depth: Breadth: Scope:

94. Moe, S.Z., Thu, Y.K., Thant, H.A., Min, N.W.: Neural Machine Translation between Myanmar Sign Language and Myanmar Written Text. In: the Second Regional Conference on Optical Character Recognition and Natural Language Processing Technologies for ASEAN Languages, pp. 13–14 (2018) Deaf involvement: no Evaluation: Level 0. Yes, data collection of 22 SL-trainers, and deaf people with different MSL dialects and different ages Level: 0 Depth: Breadth: Scope:

95. Morrissey, S. (2011). Assessing three representation methods for sign language machine translation and evaluation. In Proceedings of the 15th annual meeting of the European association for machine translation (EAMT 2011), Leuven, Belgium (pp. 137–144). Citeseer. Deaf involvement: However, the authors pointed out that, given the auto?matic evaluation used, it was not clear which was the best format and that experiments should be accompanied by human evaluation to ascertain the translation quality Evaluation: Level 0. A native ISL signer manually translated and signed the dialogue in ISL Level: 0 Depth: Breadth: Scope:

96. Müller, M., Ebling, S., Avramidis, E., Battisti, A., Berger, M., Bowden, R., Brafort, A., Cihan Camgöz, N., España-Bonet, C., Grundkiewicz, R., Jiang, Z., Koller, O., Moryossef, A., Perrollaz, R., Reinhard, S., Rios, A., Shterionov, D., Sidler-Miserez, S., Tissi, K., Van Landuyt, D.: Findings of the frst wmt shared task on sign language translation (wmt-slt22). In: Proceedings of the Seventh Conference on Machine Translation, pp. 744–772. Association for Computational Linguistics, Abu Dhabi (2022). https://aclanthology.org/2022.wmt-1.71 Deaf involvement: Seven teams participated, four native German speakers who were educated interpreters Evaluation: Level 0. Manually correction of subtitles by deaf signers, evaluators trained DGSG interpreters Level: 0 Depth: Breadth: Scope:

97. Rodriguez, J., Martinez, F.: How important is motion in sign lan- guage translation? IET Comput. Vision 15(3), 224–234 (2021) Deaf involvement: No Evaluation: Level 0. 9 deaf signers and 2 CODAs for the recordings of the dataset Level: 0 Depth: Breadth: Scope:

98. Al-Khalifa, H. S. (2010). Introducing Arabic sign language for mobile phones. In International conference on computers for handicapped persons (pp. 213–220). Springer. Deaf involvement: Evaluating of the system, not clear if the group of users were deaf. Evaluation: Five participants: 3 deaf and 2 non-deaf people answered a survey (level 1) Level: 1 Depth: Breadth: Scope:

99. Chiu, Y.-H., Wu, C.-H., Su, H.-Y., & Cheng, C.-J. (2006). Joint optimization of word alignment and epenthesis generation for Chinese to Taiwanese sign synthesis. IEEE Transactions on Pattern Analysis and Machine Intelligence, 29(1), 28–39. Deaf involvement:

Subjective evaluation (with missing how many, who are the subjects etc) Evaluation: Level 1 Five profoundly deaf students in the sixth grade evaluated the utility of the proposed approach as practical learning aid Level: 1 Depth: 5 SL users + (hearing) researchers Breadth: Little variation Scope: In the evaluation/ reflection phrase

100. Hilzensauer, M., Krammer, K.: A multilingual dictionary for sign languages:"spreadthesign". ICERI2015 Proceedings, 7826–7834 (2015) Deaf involvement: no Evaluation: Level 1. Fifteen partner countries, according to a list, which were discussed with deaf collaborators - who then chose the signs / or sign dialects Level: 1 Depth: Breadth: Scope:

101. Khan, N. S., Abid, A., & Abid, K. (2020). A novel natural language processing (NLP)– based machine translation model for English to Pakistan sign language translation. Cognitive Computation, 12, 748–765. Deaf involvement: Yes, deaf scholars for evaluation (amount is not mentioned) Evaluation: Level 1, Translating English sentences into PSL sentences with the help of SL interpreters and three deaf subjects for recordings, also used for evaluation. Level: 1 Depth: Breadth: Scope:

102. López-Ludeña, V., San-Segundo, R., Montero, J. M., Córdoba, R., Ferreiros, J., & Pardo, J. M. (2012). Automatic categorization for improving Spanish into Spanish Sign Language machine translation. Computer Speech and Language, 26(3), 149–167. Deaf involvement: Two experts in LSE, who were also involved into the corpus generation, but the authors aknowledged that deaf people also should be evaluate how the avatar represents these signs Evaluation: Level 1: These sentences were translated into LSE, both in text (sequence of signs) and in video, and compiled in an excel file. The translation was carried out by two LSE experts in parallel. When there was any discrepancy between them, a committee of four people (one Spanish linguist, 2 deaf LSE experts, and a Spanish linguistic expert on LSE) who knew LSE took the decision: select one of the LSE expert proposals, propose a new one translation alternative, or considering both proposals as alternative translations. Level: 1 Depth: Two LSE experts (for translation) , Spanish linguist, 2 deaf LSE experts and a Spanish-LSE experts Breadth: little variation but the SL-user is involved Scope: implementation, reflection

103. Luqman, H., & Mahmoud, S. A. (2019). Automatic translation of Arabic text-to-Arabic sign language. Universal Access in the Information Society, 18(4), 939–951. Deaf involvement: Yes, evaluation by 1 deaf person and 1 translator Evaluation: level 1: based on wordlist 2 native signers for translating Arabic into ArSL, evaluation by 1 deaf person and 1 expert bilingual translator Level: 1 Depth: (hearing) researchers, SL-interpreters, three deaf subjects Breadth: Little variation in the groups Scope: implementation, reflection

104. Rodriguez, J., Chacon, J., Rangel, E., Guayacan, L., Hernandez, C., Hernandez, L., Martinez, F.: Understanding motion in sign language: A new structured translation dataset. In: Proceedings of the Asian Conference on Computer Vision (2020) Deaf involvement: Yes, for training and testing of data Evaluation: Level 1. Five deaf signers out of different regios has been recorded, 10 signers for training and testing evaluation. Level: 1 Depth: Breadth: Scope:

105. Sagawa, H., Ohki, M., Sakiyama, T., Oohira, E., Ikeda, H., & Fujisawa, H. (1996). Pattern recognition and synthesis for a sign language translation system. Journal of Visual Languages and Computing, 7(1), 109–127. Deaf involvement: Yes, 1 deaf person for data-collection (level -1 or level 0) Evaluation: Four hearing-impaired and two interpreters evaluated the SL sentences (level 1) Level: 1 Depth: Only (hearing) researchers Breadth: 1 deaf person, four HoH persons, two interpreters Scope: In data-collection and evaluation

106. San-Segundo, R., López, V., Martın, R., Sánchez, D., Garcıa, A.: Language resources for Spanish–Spanish sign language (lse) translation. In: Proceedings of the 4th Workshop on the Representation and Processing of Sign Languages: Corpora and Sign Language Technologies at LREC, pp. 208–211 (2010) Deaf involvement: Yes, ten deaf signers tested the system in a real-life situation Evaluation: Level 1. the first day was an information day about the project and the evaluation, the second day within 6 different scenarios was tested. Level: 1 Depth: Only (hearing) researchers Breadth: No different groups/ variations are involved Scope: In none of the research life cycle steps

107. Stein, D., Bungeroth, J., & Ney, H. (2006). Morphosyntax based statistical methods for automatic sign language translation. In Proceedings of the 11th annual conference of the European association for machine translation. Deaf involvement: Yes, for evaluation (2 deaf people) Evaluation: Yes. For the rating of the coherence of a German sentence to the avatar output (level 1) Level: 1 Depth: 2 SL users + (hearing) researchers Breadth: Little variation Scope: In evaluation/ reflection phrase

108. Su, H.-Y., & Wu, C.-H. (2009). Improving structural statistical machine translation for sign language with small corpus using thematic role templates as translation memory. IEEE Transactions on Audio, Speech, and Language Processing, 17(7), 1305–1315. Deaf involvement: 10 deaf students (divided into control and test group) Evaluation: Level 1. The developed parallel bilingual corpus has been annotated and verified by 3 TSL linguists Level: 1 Depth: 10 deaf students divided over 2 groups, and 3 TSL linguists Breadth: Variation by two control and test groups, check by TSL linguists Scope: implementation, reflection

109. Wu, C.-H., Su, H.-Y., Chiu, Y.-H., & Lin, C.-H. (2007). Transfer-based statistical translation of Taiwanese sign language using PCFG. ACM Transactions on Asian Language Information Processing (TALIP), 6(1), 1–es. Deaf involvement: Subjective evaluation Evaluation: Level 1: group 1: 10 hearing people who used TSL for years, group 2: 10 native TSL signers evaluated the translated sentences Level: 1 Depth: 10 hearing people who used TSL for years + 10 native TSL signers + (hearing) researchers Breadth: Variation by two groups (native and non-native signers Scope: In the evaluation/ reflection phrase

110. Zhou, H., Zhou, W., Qi, W., Pu, J., & Li, H. (2021). Improving sign language translation with monolingual data by sign back-translation. In Proceedings of the IEEE/CVF conference on computer vision and pattern recognition (pp. 1316–1325). Deaf involvement: no Evaluation: level 1. SL linguistic experts, several SL teachers for design of the specific content, 10 native signers for video recording Level: 1 Depth: Breadth: Scope:

111. Jantunen, T., Rousi, R., Rainò, P., Turunen, M., Moeen Valipoor, M., & García, N. (2021). Is there any hope for developing automated translation technology for sign languages. Multilingual Facilitation, 61–73. Deaf involvement: Evaluation: Level 2. There are NADs included, and also a paragraph about Co-Engineering, Participation and Culture Level: 2 Depth: Breadth: Scope:

112. Morrissey, S., & Way, A. (2007). Joining hands: Developing a sign language machine translation system with and for the deaf community. Deaf involvement: two deaf signers for translation work anhd cosuiltation work + data-collection Evaluation: Level 2? Yes, the involvement of deaf colleagues, members of the deaf community within the choice of a domain for SLT (by asking the Centre for Deaf Studies), the human translation, advice on the SL grammar and linguistics, manual evaluators of the translated output Level: 2 Depth: deaf collegeagues + (hearing) researchers Breadth: Deaf Studies, deaf colleagues (in team) and SLC Scope: Initiation, planning, implementation, reflection

PaSCo1: A Parallel Video-SiGML Swiss French Sign Language Corpus in Medical Domain

Bastien David[1], **Pierrette Bouillon**[1], **Jonathan Mutal**[1], **Irene Strasly**[1], **Johanna Gerlach**[1] and **Hervé Spechbach**[2]

[1] TIM/FTI, University of Geneva, Geneva, Switzerland
[2] DMPR-HUG, Geneva University Hospitals, Geneva, Switzerland

Correspondence: bastien.david, pierrette.bouillon, jonathan.mutal, irene.strasly, johanna.gerlach@unige.ch
herve.spechbach@hug.ch

Abstract

This article introduces the parallel sign language translation corpus, PaSCo1, developed as part of the BabelDr project, an automatic speech translation system for medical triage. PaSCo1 aims to make a set of medical data available in Swiss French Sign Language (LSF-CH) in the form of both videos signed by a human and their description in G-SiGML mark-up language. We describe the beginnings of the corpus as part of the BabelDr project, as well as the methodology used to create the videos and generate the G-SiGML language using the SiGLA platform. The resulting FAIR corpus comprises 2 031 medical questions and instructions in the form of videos and G-SiGML code.

1 Introduction

Today, there are few corpora available for sign languages (SLs), which slows the development of data-driven systems (Table 1). The existing corpora also remain marginal compared with those developed for spoken languages. In the context of neural machine translation, Vandeghinste et al. (2024, p.122) mention that data available for the largest SL corpus (Prillwitz et al., 2008) is still 10 times smaller than its Europarl equivalent (Koehn, 2005). Some SLs are also very poorly represented, such as Swiss French Sign Language (LSF-CH, *Langue des signes française de Suisse romande*)[1].

There are several problems that make the development of SL corpora difficult. SLs are not written languages and SL corpora are mainly stored in video format. Also, many of these corpora contain interpreted speeches. They are therefore rarely parallel to the originals, which makes it difficult to align the source and the target texts. In addition, the large number of signers in general leads to dialectal variation and a lack of uniformity in the language. The collection and annotation of SL corpora is also longer than for their spoken equivalents with the lack of flexibility in the editing and post-production work on some videos further extending the working time. Finally, the recording format used may become obsolete after a few years and conversion to another standard is not always possible, leading to the loss of recorded data (Chiriac et al., 2016).

To annotate videos, a writing system that is descriptive and machine-readable has several advantages. It can be easily manipulated, adapted, and interpreted, unlike data from video recordings. G-SiGML (Elliott et al., 2004), for example, is an XML mark-up language based on the Hamburg Notation System for Sign Languages (HamNoSys) (Hanke, 2004). It is composed of several levels of information specific to SLs and is able to control a JASigning virtual animation (Ebling and Glauert, 2013). This code has also been used as a pivot for the development of machine translation and annotation systems, for example in Skobov and Lepage (2020) or Mutal et al. (2024).

In this paper, we present PaSCo1[2], a corpus translating French medical triage questions and instructions into LSF-CH, composed of human-signed videos and the corresponding G-SiGML code. We introduce the French source corpus (section 2) and the different SL translation methodologies (section 3) before describing the content of the corpus (section 4) and its public metadata.

[1]In 2023, there were almost 20 000 deaf people will live in Switzerland, 20 % of them in French-speaking cantons (Boyes-Braem and Rathmann, 2010). The canton of XXX is currently the only French-speaking canton that recognizes LSF-CH in its constitution.

[2]PaSCo1 repository: https://doi.org/10/gqnbps, consulted on April 24, 2025.

Proceedings of the Third International Workshop on Automatic Translation for Signed and Spoken Languages (AT4SSL), pages 37–43, June 24, 2025

Dataset	Reference		Recording		Area
	Date	Author	Human	G-SiGML	
GSLC	2007	Efthimiou and Fotinea	Yes	No	Education
NGT-Corpus	2008	Crasborn and Zwitserlood	Yes	No	N/S
DGS-Korpus	2008	Prillwitz et al.	Yes	No	N/S
RWTH-Phoenix	2012	Forster et al.	Yes	No	Weather
Dicta-Sign	2012	Matthes et al.	Yes	No	Travel
DGS-Corpus	2020	Hanke et al.	Yes	No	N/S
GSL Dataset	2020	Adaloglou et al.	Yes	No	Service
BOBSL	2021	Albanie et al.	Yes	No	N/S
OpenASL	2022	Shi et al.	Yes	No	N/S
Youtube-ASL	2023	Uthus et al.	Yes	No	N/S
PaSCo1	**2024**	**David et al.**	**Yes**	**Yes**	**Health**

Table 1: Some Examples of Public SL Corpora

2 Source corpus

The source corpus (language: French) was developed for the BabelDr[3] translation application as part of a collaboration between the Faculty of Translation and Interpreting (FTI) and the Outpatient emergency unit of the primary care medicine ward in Geneva University Hospitals (HUG), supported by the HUG private foundation (Rayner et al., 2016).

BabelDr is a fixed-sentence translation system. It is based on 11 089 sentences pre-translated by humans linked to more than a million variants using a grammar (Bouillon et al., 2021). The translation system works in four stages: (1) the doctor asks a question orally, (2) the system uses speech recognition to recognize the sentence, (3) as in a translation memory, the result of the speech recognition is linked to the closest sentence in the database using neural methods trained on the synthetic corpus generated by the grammar: (4) if the doctor validates this result, the sentence is then finally shown to the non-native speaker patient.

The source corpus has already been translated into written and spoken forms in 11 different languages (Arabic, Algerian Arabic, Moroccan Arabic, Tunisian Arabic, Dari, Farsi, Russian, Simple English, Spanish, Tigrigna and Ukrainian). A partial version in LSF-CH has been added using human-recorded videos and avatar animations. The aim was to be able to compare users' perceptions of these two modalities, in terms of usability and more specifically patient satisfaction, a very important criterion in medicine for adherence to treatment, for example Janakiram et al. (2020) and David et al. (2022b). The following section describes the translation methodology used to translate the French source corpus into SL.

[3]BabelDr website: https://babeldr.unige.ch/, consulted on Avril 24, 2025

3 Translation methodology

The translation methodology follows a two-step process. First, a set of reference recordings is produced by human translators (section 3.1). These reference translations are then used to generate the G-SiGML code using a rule-based approach (section 3.2).

3.1 Reference translation

The LSF-CH reference translations were produced in a recording studio at the University of Geneva. The team consisted of a deaf nurse, a hearing doctor, a hearing interpreter and two deaf LSF-CH experts who all worked collaboratively to produce the final videos. Following team discussions, the deaf nurse was filmed for the final version of the translations (Strasly et al., 2018).

The recording was done using the LiteDevTool online platform, which enables the video content to be stored immediately and avoids any post-production work. The captured video stream is displayed, validated and then recorded in real time (Gerlach et al., 2018). During the translation process, three deaf individuals from the local deaf community—who are also LSF-CH teachers—regularly came to the university to ensure the translated content was accurate and easy to understand. After the initial set of translations was filmed, the project coordinator held seven focus groups with members of the local deaf community to gather feedback, which was then used to refine existing translations and adapt the additional content that had to be added to the existing corpus (Strasly, 2024).

3.2 Translation into animation

The second phase of the project was to develop the G-SiGML code for the reference corpus. This mark-up language can be used to generate a fully synthesized animation.

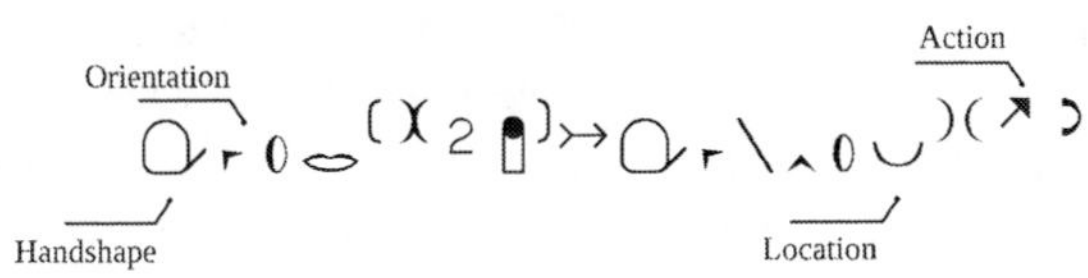

Figure 1: Lexical Resource: HamNosys Notation [HELLO - LSF-CH]

The code was generated using SIGLA,[4] a web-based application developed to generate G-SiGML code from a glossary and translation grammar (David et al., 2022c).

SIGLA has a storage function (GLOSSARY and GRAMMAR) and a code generation and animation function (GENERATE).

The GLOSSARY feature loads and stores lexical data written using the Hamburg Notation System for Sign Languages (HAMNOSYS) (Prillwitz et al., 1989), a phonological language notation system describing the physical components of each hand gesture. Figure 1 shows the phonological composition (hand shape, palm and finger orientation, location and movement) of the sign HELLO (LSF-CH) in HAMNOSYS. For the BabelDr project, 608 glosses/HAMNOSYS entries were manually produced: 370 nouns, 82 actions, 57 adjectives, 36 adverbs, 19 transfer signs, 15 pronouns, 8 prepositions, 5 forms of punctuation, 3 interjections and 3 conjugation terms.

The GRAMMAR feature loads and stores synchronous context-free grammar rules. A rule is multi-channel and maps sentences to the appropriate sequence of glosses/ HAMNOSYS entries. Each gloss is synchronized to different non-manual channels and lip expressions that are pre-registered in G-SiGML. Each rule can also introduce terminal or non-terminal variables. Our grammar resource contains nearly 450 rules, 115 non-terminal symbols and 608 terminals. Several grammatical and lexical sets can be loaded onto SIGLA.

Users can load the stored lexical and grammatical content they require, as well as the rule they wish to translate, using the GENERATE functionality. SIGLA then transforms the rule into the sign table (Rayner et al., 2016), the intermediate representation of the synchronized signed sentence. The matrix in figure 2 shows an example of a grammar rule with the corresponding sign table for the sentence "Hello, I am the nurse". This sign table is then translated into G-SiGML notation (Elliott et al., 2004). The gloss encodes individual sign features from the HAMNOSYS, while the other lines represent pre-registered non-manual features. In addition to the G-SiGML code corresponding to the rule, the generation output includes a JASigning animation, the translation in written format and the sign table.

Once this process is completed, the G-SiGML codes are imported into the BabelDr in CSV format. Each new import overwrites the previous one in order to match the latest corrections made in the initial resources. The grammar can now generate 1 234 828 synthetically signed sentences, 6 200 of which have been imported into BabelDr.

4 Parallel Sign language Corpus (PaSCo1)

The PaSCo1[5] corpus has been available since August 2022 though the institutional repository YARETA. Respecting the FAIR principles of access to information, the data can be downloaded easily and securely.

This corpus makes our medical data available in formats adapted to sign language. It is characterized by two features:

- **Domain**: Unlike many sign language corpora, PaSCo1 specializes in the medical field. It translates a set of questions and instructions related to the medical emergency context.
- **Composition**: PaSCo1 is a parallel corpus composed of French triage questions, LSF-CH videos and the corresponding descriptions in G-SiGML.

[4]SIGLA application: https://babeldr.unige.ch/demos-and-resources#sigla, consulted on May 24, 2025.

[5]PaSCo1 repository: https://doi.org/10/gqnbps, consulted on April 24, 2025.

Utterance			
Source	Hello, I am **$$the_staff**		
Gloss	HELLO	I-AM	**$$the_staff**
Aperture	Wide	Wide	**$$the_staff**
Gaze	Down	Neutral	**$$the_staff**
Head	Up	Neutral	**$$the_staff**
Mouthing	hi	im	**$$the_staff**
EndUtterance			

→

Gloss	HELLO	I-AM	NURSE
Aperture	Wide	Wide	Closed
Gaze	Down	Neutral	Up
Head	Up	Neutral	Neutral
Mouthing	hi	im	nurse

Figure 2: Grammar Resource: Translation Rule and Sign Table [I am the nurse - LSF-CH]

Corpus	1	2	3
BabelDr	N:11 089	N:82 152	N:2 260
PaSCo1	N:2 031 %:18,3	N:17 023 %:20,7	N:833 %:36,8

Table 2: Number (N) of Sentences (1), Tokens (2) and Types (3) in the BabelDr and PaSCo1 Source Corpus

PaSCo1 consists of two sub-folders containing 2 031 MP4 files. The first sub-folder contains the reference translations which correspond to almost 5 hours of video recordings, while the second contains the corresponding G-SiGMLs. A README file is attached to the main folder and provides the correspondences between the source sentences (*"Do you take vitamins every day?"*), the standardized names of the video files (*BabelDr_LSFCH_1804*), the G-SiGML notations and subtitle files.

18,3 % of the sentences in the BabelDr source corpus are now available in PaSCo1 (Table 2). At the lexical level, this represents 20,7 % of all words (tokens) and 36,8 % of unique words present (types). The corpus contains 20 181 gloss tokens, which means an average of 9,9 glosses per sentence.

Table 3 shows the distribution of the 2 031 sentences in PaSCo1 according to BabelDr's domains. Some sentences may belong to several domains. For example, PaSCo1 translated nearly 62,71 % of the sentences in the COVID domain, 38,87 % in checkup and 32,51 % in traumatology.

Comparing file sizes, the size of the video recordings is 5,6 GB, while the file containing the G-SiGML animation codes is just 0,02 GB. The total size needed to store the recordings should reach 30,5 GB, while a complete file of G-SiGML translations should not exceed 0,1 GB.

5 Conclusion

PaSCo1 is a French sign language medical translation corpus from French-speaking Switzerland (LSF-CH). It provides access to a set of phrases commonly used by emergency doctors when triaging patients, which are available in both video and G-SiGML formats. The latter was produced using the SIGLA platform, which generates the code, as well as the animation with a grammar and lexicon.

This corpus enables several research possibilities, including the descriptive analysis of videos in SLs, the automatic construction of virtual avatars driven by G-SiGML, the comparison of human recordings and virtual animation, the evaluation of virtual animation in the medical context and the automation of annotation in G-SiGML.

The remainder of the G-SiGML codes are already available on the BabelDr platform and will be available on YARETA soon. Currently, 1 730 selected new sentences are being translated by a team of deaf students from the University of Geneva's LSF-CH academic translation programme and will be added to the reference corpus.[6]

References

Nikolas Adaloglou, Theocharis Chatzis, Ilias Papastratis, Andreas Stergioulas, Georgios Th. Papadopoulos, Vassia Zacharopoulou, George J. Xydopoulos, Klimnis Atzakas, Dimitris Papazachariou, and Petros Daras. 2022. A Comprehensive Study on Deep Learning-Based Methods for Sign Language Recognition. *IEEE Transactions on Multimedia*, 24:1750 – 1762.

Samuel Albanie, Gül Varol, Liliane Momeni, Hannah Bull, Triantafyllos Afouras, Himel Chowdhury, Neil Fox, Bencie Woll, Rob Cooper, Andrew McParland, and Andrew Zisserman. 2021. BBC-Oxford British Sign Language Dataset.

Pierrette Bouillon, Johanna Gerlach, Jonathan Mutal, Nikos Tsourakis, and Hervé Spechbach. 2021. A

[6]UNIGE page: https://perma.cc/ZD3B-3E22, consulted on April 24, 2025

Domain	Source Corpus			PaSCo1		
	1	2	3	1	2	3
Checkup	N:4 784	N:39 471	N:1 737	N:1 862 %:38,87	N:15 647 %:39,64	N:747 %:43,00
Chest	N:4 721	N:39 217	N:1 720	N:1 269 %:26,87	N:10 530 %:26,85	N:714 %:41,51
Covid	N:236	N:1 435	N:348	N:148 %:62,71	N:934 %:65,08	N:293 %:84,19
Traumatology	N:3 325	N:26 958	N:1 524	N:1 081 %:32,51	N:8 745 %:32,43	N:643 %:42,19
Follow-up	N:1 551	N:13 316	N:1 051	N:242 %:15,60	N:1 583 %:11,88	N:412 %:39,20
Dermatology	N:3 682	N:31 082	N:1 594	N:940 %:25,52	N:7 622 %:24,52	N:660 %:41,40
Habits	N:1 273	N:11 440	N:745	N:60 %:4,71	N:431 %:3,76	N:146 %:19,59
Abdomen	N:7 094	N:59 219	N:1 846	N:1 987 %:28,00	N:16 728 %:28,24	N:823 %:44,58
Head	N:5 399	N:43 403	N:1 781	N:1 255 %:23,24	N:10 270 %:23,66	N:723 %:40,59

Table 3: Number (N) of Sentences (1), Tokens (2) and Types (3) in the BabelDr Source Corpus and PaSCo1

Speech-enabled Fixed-phrase Translator for Healthcare Accessibility. In *Proceedings of the 1st Workshop on NLP for Positive Impact*, NLP4PI 2021, pages 135 – 142, Online. Association for Computational Linguistics (ACL).

Penny Boyes-Braem and Christian Rathmann. 2010. Transmission of Sign Languages in Northern Europe. In Diane Brentari, editor, *Cambridge Language Surveys: Sign Languages*, pages 19 – 45. Cambridge University Press, Cambridge.

Ionut A. Chiriac, Lăcrămioara Stoicu-Tivadar, and Elena Podoleanu. 2016. Romanian Sign Language Oral Health Corpus in Video and Animated Avatar Technology. In Valentina E. Balas, Lakhmi C. Jain, and Branko Kovačević, editors, *Soft Computing Applications*, volume 356 of *Advances in Intelligent Systems and Computing*, pages 279 – 293. Springer, Cham.

Onno Crasborn and Inge Zwitserlood. 2008. The Corpus NGT: An Online Corpus for Professionals and Laymen. In *Proceedings of the 3rd Workshop on the Representation and Processing of Sign Languages*, LREC 2008, pages 44 – 49, Marrakech, Morocco. European Language Resources Association (ELRA).

Bastien David, Pierrette Bouillon, Irene Strasly, Jonathan Mutal, Johanna Gerlach, and Hervé Spechbach. 2022a. Parallel Sign Language Corpus.

Bastien David, Jonathan Mutal, Irene Strasly, Pierrette Bouillon, and Hervé Spechbach. 2022b. Babeldr: un système de traduction du discours médical vers l'animation virtuelle signée. In *12e conférence de l'IFRATH sur les technologies d'assistance*, Handicap 2022, Paris, France. IFRATH.

Bastien David, Jonathan Mutal, Irene Strasly, Johanna Gerlach, and Pierrette Bouillon. 2022c. SIGLA: une plateforme de développement d'animations en langue des signes. In *Technologies du Langage Humain et Accès Interactif à l'Information*, TLH-JAII 2022, pages 22 – 24, Paris, France.

Sarah Ebling and John Glauert. 2013. Exploiting the Full Potential of JASigning to Build an Avatar Signing Train Announcements. In *Third International Symposium on Sign Language Translation and Avatar Technology*, SLTAT 2023, Chicago, IL, USA. s.n.

Eleni Efthimiou and Stavroula-Evita Fotinea. 2007. GSLC: Creation and annotation of a Greek sign language corpus for HCI. In Constantine Stephanidis, editor, *Universal Access in Human Computer Interaction*, volume 4554 of *Lecture Notes in Computer Science*, pages 657 – 666. Springer, Berlin, Heidelberg.

Ralph Elliott, John Glauert, Vince Jennings, and Richard Kennaway. 2004. An Overview of the SiGML Notation and SiGMLSigning Software System. In *Proceedings of the 1st Workshop on the Representation and Processing of Sign Languages*, LREC 2004, pages 98 – 104, Lisbon, Portugal. European Language Resources Association (ELRA).

Jens Forster, Christoph Schmidt, Thomas Hoyoux, Oscar Koller, Uwe Zelle, Justus Piater, and Hermann Ney. 2012. RWTH-PHOENIX-Weather: A Large Vocabulary Sign Language Recognition and Translation Corpus. In *Proceedings of the Eighth International Conference on Language Resources and Evaluation*, LREC 2012, pages 3785 – 3789, Istanbul, Turkey. European Language Resources Association (ELRA).

Johanna Gerlach, Hervé Spechbach, and Pierrette Bouillon. 2018. Creating an Online Translation Platform to Build Target Language Resources for a Medical Phraselator. In *40th Conference on Translating and the Computer*, TC40, pages 60 – 65, London, UK. AsLing.

Thomas Hanke. 2004. HamNoSys: Representing sign language data in language ressources and language processing contexts. In *Proceedings of the 1st Workshop on the Representation and Processing of Sign Languages*, LREC 2004, Lisbon, Portugal. European Language Resources Association (ELRA).

Thomas Hanke, Marc Schulder, Reiner Konrad, and Elena Jahn. 2020. Extending the Public DGS Corpus in size and depth. In *Proceedings of the 9th Workshop on the Representation and Processing of Sign Languages*, LREC 2020, pages 75 – 82, Marseille, France. European Language Resources Association (ELRA).

Antony A. Janakiram, Johanna Gerlach, Alyssa Vuadens-Lehmann, Pierrette Bouillon, and Hervé Spechbach. 2020. User Satisfaction with a Speech-Enabled Translator in Emergency Settings. *Studies in Health Technology and Informatics*, 270:1421 – 1422.

Philipp Koehn. 2005. Europarl: A Parallel Corpus for Statistical Machine Translation. In *Proceedings of Machine Translation Summit X*, MTSummit 2005, pages 79 – 86, Phuket, Thailand.

Silke Matthes, Thomas Hanke, Anja Regen, Jakob Storz, Satu Worseck, Eleni Efthimiou, Athanasia-Lida Dimou, Annelies Braffort, John Glauert, and Eva Safar. 2012. Dicta-Sign: Building a Multilingual Sign Language Corpus. In *Proceedings of the 5th Workshop on the Representation and Processing of Sign Languages*, LREC 2012, pages 117 – 122, Istanbul, Turkey. European Language Resources Association (ELRA).

Jonathan D. Mutal, Raphael Rubino, Pierrette Bouillon, Bastien David, Johanna Gerlach, and Irene Strasly. 2024. Improving sign language production in the healthcare domain using UMLS and multi-task learning. In *Proceedings of the 1st Workshop on Patient-Oriented Language Processing*, LREC-COLING 2024, pages 1–7, Torino, Italia. European Language Resources Association (ELRA).

Siegmund Prillwitz, Thomas Hanke, Susanne König, Reiner Konrad, Gabriele Langer, and Arvid Schwarz. 2008. DGS Corpus Project: Development of a Corpus Based Electronic Dictionary German Sign Language / German. In *Proceedings of the 3rd Workshop on the Representation and Processing of Sign Languages*, LREC 2008, pages 159 – 164, Marrakech, Morocco. European Language Resources Association (ELRA).

Siegmund Prillwitz, Regina Leven, Heiko Zienert, Thomas Hanke, and Jan Henning. 1989. *Hamburg Notation System for Sign Languages: An Introductory Guide*, volume 5 of *International Studies on Sign Language and the Communication of the Deaf.* Signum, Hamburg, Germany.

Manny Rayner, Alejandro Armando, Pierrette Bouillon, Sarah Ebling, Johanna Gerlach, Sonia Halimi, Irene Strasly, and Nikos Tsourakis. 2016. Helping Domain Experts Build Phrasal Speech Translation Systems. In José F. Quesada, Francisco-Jesús Martín Mateos, and Teresa Lopez-Soto, editors, *Future and Emergent Trent in Language Technology*, volume 9577 of *Lecture Notes in Artificial Intelligence*, pages 41 – 52. Springer, Cham.

Bowen Shi, Diane Brentari, Gregory Shakhnarovich, and Karen Livescu. 2022. Open-Domain Sign Language Translation Learned from Online Video. In *Proceedings of the 2022 Conference on Empirical Methods in Natural Language Processing*, pages 6365 – 6379, Abu Dhabi, United Arab Emirates. Association for Computational Linguistics (ACL).

Victor Skobov and Yves Lepage. 2020. Video-to-HamNoSys Automated Annotation System. In *Proceedings of the 9th Workshop on the Representation and Processing of Sign Languages*, LREC 2020, pages 209 – 216, Marseille, France. European Language Resources Association (ELRA).

Irene Strasly. 2024. *De la traduction médicale sur le terrain à la formation universitaire : étude de cas par la recherche-action sur la communauté sourde et la langue des signes française de Suisse romande.* Ph.D. thesis, Université de Genève.

Irene Strasly, Tanya Sebaï, Evelyne Rigot, Valentin Marti, Jesus Manuel Gonzalez, Johanna Gerlach, Hervé Spechbach, and Pierrette Bouillon. 2018. Le projet BabelDr: Rendre les informations médicales accessibles en langue des signes de Suisse romande (LSF-SR). In *Proceedings of the 2nd Swiss Conference on Barrier-free Communication*, BfC 2018, pages 92 – 96, Geneva.

David Uthus, Garrett Tanzer, and Manfred Georg. 2023. YouTube-ASL: A Large-Scale, Open-Domain American Sign Language-English Parallel Corpus. In *Proceedings of the 37th International Conference on*

Neural Information Processing Systems, NIPS 2023, Red Hook, NY, USA. Curran Associates Inc.

Vincent Vandeghinste, Mirella De Sisto, Santiago Egea Gómez, and Mathieu De Coster. 2024. Challenges with Sign Language Datasets. In Andy Way, Lorraine Leeson, and Dimitar Shterionov, editors, *Sign Language Machine Translation*, volume 5 of *Machine Translation: Technologies and Applications*, pages 117 – 139. Springer, Cham.

Author Index

Association for Computational Linguistics
209 N. Eighth Street
Stroudsburg, Pennsylvania 18360

ISBN 979-8-3313-2670-8

CURRAN ASSOCIATES INC.
proceedings.com